ORTHO'S All About

Ground Covers

Written by Katie Lamar Smith

Meredith® Books
Des Moines, Iowa

Ortho® Books
An imprint of Meredith® Books

All About Ground Covers
Writer: Katie Lamar Smith
Editor: Marilyn Rogers
Technical Consultant: Harrison Flint
Art Director: Tom Wegner
Assistant Art Director: Harijs Priekulis
Copy Chief: Catherine Hamrick
Copy and Production Editor: Terri Fredrickson
Book Production Managers: Pam Kvitne,
    Marjorie J. Schenkelberg
Contributing Copy Editors: Chardel Gibson Blaine, Angela
    K. Renkoski, Barbara Feller-Roth
Contributing Proofreaders: Fran Gardner, Beth Lastine,
    Kenya McCullum
Contributing Prop/Photo Stylist: Peggy Johnston
Indexer: Donald Glassman
Electronic Production Coordinator: Paula Forest
Editorial and Design Assistants: Kathleen Stevens,
    Karen Schirm

Additional Editorial Contributions from
    Art Rep Services
Director: Chip Nadeau
Designers: lk Design
Illustrators: Dave Brandon, Shawn Wallace

Meredith® Books
Editor in Chief: James D. Blume
Design Director: Matt Strelecki
Managing Editor: Gregory H. Kayko
Executive Ortho Editor: Larry Erickson

Director, Retail Sales and Marketing: Terry Unsworth
Director, Sales, Special Markets: Rita McMullen
Director, Sales, Premiums: Michael A. Peterson
Director, Sales, Retail: Tom Wierzbicki
Director, Sales, Home & Garden Centers: Ray Wolf
Director, Book Marketing: Brad Elmitt
Director, Operations: George A. Susral
Director, Production: Douglas M. Johnston

Vice President, General Manager: Jamie L. Martin

Meredith Publishing Group
President, Publishing Group: Christopher M. Little
Vice President, Finance & Administration: Max Runciman

Meredith Corporation
Chairman and Chief Executive Officer: William T. Kerr
Chairman of the Executive Committee: E.T. Meredith III

Katie Lamar Smith is a writer for the Alabama Experiment
Station and College of Agriculture at Auburn University.
Harrison Flint is professor emeritus in the Department of
Horticulture at Purdue University.

Thanks to
Janet Anderson, Paula Clemow, Charles Ewald,
    Heard Gardens

Photographers
(Photographers credited may retain copyright ©
to the listed photographs.)
L = Left, R = Right, C = Center, B = Bottom, T = Top
Liz Ball/Positive Images: 48T; **Jim Baron/The Image
Finders:** 11B, 52; **Kate Boykin:** 55T, 77B; **Karen
Bussolini/Positive Images:** 56B, 89B; **Rob Cardillo:** 6, 15,
22L, 22C, 22R, 25, 29, 30T, 35, 40, 43T; **David Cavagnaro:**
74C, 77T, 80T; **Alan Copeland:** 28B, 30B; **Barbara J.
Coxe:** 13B; **Crandall & Crandall:** 45; **Thomas E. Eltzroth:**
85T; **Derek Fell:** 24, 48C, 58C, 59C, 63T, 64B, 67C, 73B,
79B, 90C, 91B; **John Glover:** 17C, 21T, 58T, 62B, 65T,
69B, 70T, 70B, 71T, 71B, 73T, 73C, 81B, 83C, 88T, 90B;
David Goldberg: 27, 50, 51T; **Harry Haralambou/ Positive
Images:** 54C; **Jerry Harpur:** 10B, 11T, 12, 82B; **Lynne
Harrison:** 31, 56T, 87C; **Saxon Holt:** 9T, 9B, 20TR, 43B,
56C, 60T, 61T, 61C, 63C, 63B, 75T, 78T, 81T, 82T, 83T,
87B; **Jerry Howard/Positive Images:** 19T, 46, 87T; **Bill
Johnson:** 80C; **Michael Landis:** 32, 38, 86T; **Andrew
Lawson:** 60B, 61B, 75C, 77C; **Janet Loughrey:** 10T, 71C;
Brian McCay: 14T, 28T; **David McDonald:** 66C, 85B;
Alan Majchrowicz: 13T; **Clive Nichols:** 65B, **Clive
Nichols/Copton Ash, Kent:** 76B; **Arthur N.
Orans/Horticultural Photography:** 55C; **Jerry Pavia:** 4, 5B,
17B,18T, 20B, 64T, 67T, 69T, 70C, 72T, 74B, 79T, 82C;
Ben Phillips/Positive Images: 20TL, 48B, 62C, 66B;
Richard Shiell: 18B, 54B, 55B, 57C, 58B, 59T, 59B, 60C,
62T, 64C, 65C, 66T, 68C, 69C, 74T, 76T, 76C, 83B, 84C,
84B, 86C, 90T, 91T; **Pam Spaulding/Positive Images:** 68T;
Steve Struse: 14B, 34T, 34B, 36T, 36C, 39T, 39B, 47, 49,
51B; **Rick Taylor:** 23; **The Studio Central:** 44T, 44B;
Michael S. Thompson: 5T, 8, 13C, 17T, 54T, 57B, 68B,
72B, 78B, 80B, 81C, 84T, 85C, 86B, 88C, 88B, 89T;
Connie Toops: 67B, 78C

On the cover: Low-growing creepers, such as sandwort, Irish
moss, and baby tears, frame a path of native stone.
Photograph by Deidra Walpole.

All of us at Ortho® Books are dedicated to providing you
with the information and ideas you need to enhance your
home and garden. We welcome your comments and
suggestions about this book. Write to us at:
    Meredith Corporation
    Ortho Books
    1716 Locust St.
    Des Moines, IA 50309–3023

If you would like more information on other Ortho
products, call 800-225-2883 or visit us at www.ortho.com

GROUND COVERS IN THE LANDSCAPE 4

SELECTING GROUND COVERS 12

GROWING GROUND COVERS 24

PLANT SELECTION GUIDE 52

GROUND COVERS
IN THE LANDSCAPE

Beautiful landscapes, whether on sweeping country estates, in roomy suburban neighborhoods, on compact city lots, or even in thriving business districts, all possess one similarity—a sense of harmony and flow. One key to achieving harmony is the use of a group of versatile and adaptable plants: ground covers.

Ground covers are often inconspicuous elements of a landscape; they blend in so well that you may overlook their many uses and benefits. But these unassuming plants are the workhorses of the landscape, meeting many needs. They solve scores of design and landscape management problems, reduce maintenance requirements, and add diversity and contrast to your landscape. They furnish a transition between lofty trees and low lawns, and relieve monotony in your yard as they change with the seasons. What's more, ground covers include a wide range of plant types—evergreen to deciduous, flowering and nonflowering, creeping or upright. There is a ground cover plant available for virtually any setting, need, or climate.

Establishing ground covers requires some initial effort, but the energy and imagination you invest will be rewarded with a vibrant, functional, and enduring landscape.

Ground covers serve many functions in a landscape, and one of the most common is unity. These diverse, low-growing plants help make the transition from taller trees to medium-sized shrubs to lawns or hardscapes. Here, sedum provides the unifying element to make a graceful and handsome landscape. From this photo, you can see that no matter what climate you live in, there is a ground cover to do the job.

WHAT ARE GROUND COVERS?

For centuries, ground-covering plants have cloaked the earth's surface with a natural carpet of vegetation, protecting and nurturing the soil. These plants have adapted to their environments, thriving in the most formidable climates and the poorest soils. Generations of agriculturists have used ground covers to conserve and enrich the soil; nowadays, homeowners and landscapers plant them for various purposes in ornamental settings.

Technically, ground covers include a wide range of materials—both living and nonliving—that blanket the soil, protecting it from erosion and degradation. Turfgrass, the best-known and most commonly used living ornamental ground cover, is ideal for certain settings, but it has limitations. Nonliving ground covers, such as pine bark and other organic mulches, and even stones or concrete, also have their place in landscapes. But they provide less visual variety and offer fewer soil-enhancing benefits than living ground covers.

Ground covers provide both formal and informal enhancements to a landscape. In this garden, juniper, English ivy, and St. Johnswort give a formal, manicured look to the front yard.

NATURAL GROUND COVERS

All plants can be considered ground covers because they all help secure and sustain soil. For our purposes, however, ground covers are plants that exhibit low or horizontal growth habits, spread rapidly, and protect the soil from erosion. They include plants that naturally—or with minimal pruning or mowing—range in height from less than 1 inch up to 3 feet tall. Other than that, the term "ground cover" has few restrictions in this book.

The plants that fit these criteria include a variety of materials, from woody shrubs to herbaceous succulents to herbs to vines to ferns and grasses. Among them are plants that are specifically suited for certain growing conditions, such as wet shade, as well as plants that are adapted to a wide range of environments, such as desert climates.

Ground cover options are so diverse that choosing the right one for your setting may seem overwhelming. However, once you understand the roles that ground covers can play in your landscape and the niches that specific ground covers can fill, you should have no trouble finding the right one for your needs.

The first part of this book will guide you through the process of analyzing your landscape to determine what its needs are and where ground covers will work best. Then it will help you select ground covers to match. The book winds up with a detailed encyclopedia of ground covers, guaranteed to whet your appetite.

Ground cover junipers, such as 'Tamariscifolia' savin juniper, provide a pleasing complement to taller evergreens.

FUNCTION FIRST

Many herbaceous ground covers root along their stems to form a dense soil-holding network of roots. They also tend to have showier foliage and flowers than woody plants.

Ground cover plants protect and enhance soil. They control erosion both by holding the soil in place with their web of roots and by forming a solid sheet of vegetation over the soil's surface, preventing rain or wind from dislodging soil particles. Their roots, stems, branches, and leaves also help improve soil quality by making the soil more porous and fertile through the natural process of growth and renewal.

PROTECTING SOIL FROM BELOW

Working out of sight in the ground, roots benefit the soil in a variety of ways. Botanically speaking, there are two major types of roots—taproots and fibrous roots. Fibrous roots form many tiny rootlets that spread into the soil like a web from the crown of the plant (the point at which roots and stems diverge) or from larger roots. Taproots are comprised of one large main root from which smaller rootlets may sprout.

Plants with fibrous roots are effective soil-holding ground covers because they have many small rootlets that form a dense web to hold and penetrate the soil. Plants with fibrous roots also tend to grow and spread rapidly. Their roots colonize a large area and their foliage shields the soil surface. Such plants quickly stabilize slopes and other erosion-prone areas needing rapid cover.

Taprooted plants have a more coarse root system, which takes longer to fill the soil. Even though they make effective ground covers, they're not the best choice for erosion-prone areas needing rapid cover.

Some plants, such as ivies, not only have a fibrous central root, they also form additional roots along their stems as they trail across the soil's surface, providing extra soil-holding power.

IMPROVING POROSITY

Besides binding soil particles in place, plant roots enhance soil quality by increasing porosity. Porosity encourages fertility and productivity by opening up the soil so that water readily moves through it and both oxygen and water are present in the soil's pores. With oxygen available, plants are better able to take up water and nutrients.

FROM ABOVE

Above ground, the stems, branches, and foliage of ground covers protect and enhance the soil by forming a sheltering canopy. Some ground covers, such as junipers, produce thick limbs that simply lie on the soil surface.

Woody ground covers offer permanent visual structure in the landscape. Some also bloom, fruit, and have colorful foliage. Their branches are less likely to root, instead creating a physical barrier to protect soil from erosion.

Others, such as ajuga and other herbaceous ground covers, cling to the soil, holding it together from above as well as shielding the surface. Still others, such as herbs and grasses, create a dense carpet of individual plants.

Leaves and stems control erosion when they break the force of raindrops and wind. They also check the flow of water and wind across the soil surface. In addition, these aboveground plant parts provide a barrier between the soil and the sun, which keeps the soil moist and restricts weed growth.

AIDING SOIL FERTILITY

As leaves, old roots, and other plant parts are shed from the ground covers, they collect on and in the soil, decompose, and turn into humus, which is simply decomposed organic matter. This process adds nutrients, beneficial microorganisms, and organic matter to the soil. Ground cover foliage also collects leaves and other organic debris from nearby plants,

often hiding it from view as it decomposes and is returned to the soil. This mulches your landscape and reduces the need to rake and apply additional fertilizers.

SUPPRESSING WEEDS

The foliage of most ground covers is dense enough to block sunlight from reaching the soil surface, which prevents some weed seeds from germinating. Once ground covers form a solid mat across the soil surface, they shade or crowd out most unwanted plants and discourage the invasion of new weeds. Understand, however, that only established ground covers are effective weed suppressors, and it usually takes one to three growing seasons for them to become established. You'll need to make an extra effort to keep weeds under control while ground covers mature, but once they are established, you can get by with weeding only occasionally.

Fibrous root systems hold the soil in place by forming a web or mat that binds soil particles. As the roots permeate the soil, they increase its porosity.

Stems and leaves of ground covers blanket the soil with foliage, shielding it from wind and rain erosion. Stems and foliage also insulate the soil from heat and sun, restricting weed growth and keeping the soil moist.

PROBLEM SOLVERS

In addition to protecting and enhancing the soil, ground covers reduce the amount of labor needed to maintain a beautiful landscape.

For example, once you have installed perennial ground covers—plants that live for more than two years—you rarely need to replant the area again. Also, ground cover plants often require less pruning, mowing, watering, and fertilizing than other landscape plants, because they are naturally hardy and low-growing. A ground cover bed filled with plants that are adapted to your growing conditions will thrive with minimal care.

LIVING WITH ADVERSITY

Many, though not all, ground cover plants thrive in poor soil and imperfect growing conditions, such as erodible slopes or shady areas. For example, cast-iron plant, hosta, and various ferns thrive in deep shade where turfgrass will not grow. They beautify the area and reduce mowing where protruding tree roots might damage your lawn mower blade. If there is a spot in your landscape that is too wet to grow a lawn, plants such as Chinese astilbe or bergenia can fill the void. In an arid climate or an area that is difficult to irrigate, Scotch heather, rock rose, and other drought-tolerant ground covers may thrive. Even if you live in a severe climate, such as along an ocean shore or in frigid regions where only the toughest landscape plants survive, there are ground covers that will fit your specific needs.

Ground covers can also improve safety in the landscape. For example, mowing a steep slope can be a dangerous practice. Even with a safety shutoff on the mower, slipping on wet grass could seriously injure you. Planting ground covers, such as akebia, cotoneaster, or manzanita, instead of turfgrass, on a steep area will eliminate that danger.

HELPFUL HABITATS

Ground covers also provide habitat and cover for beneficial insects and other predators, such as frogs, toads, and lizards, that control pests in the landscape. Although ground covers sometimes create an ideal habitat for slugs, snails, and other pests, this problem can be offset by the presence of the beneficial creatures. If certain pests are a particular problem in your area, plant ground covers that resist the pests.

On severe slopes that are likely to erode, ground covers can be the solution. Terraces tame the steep drop while ground covers hold the soil in place and beautify this slope. In California and other fire-prone regions, fire-retardant ground covers can protect your home.

FIREBREAKS

Some ground cover plants, especially those with a high moisture content, can serve as firebreaks, which is especially useful if you live in an arid region where wildfires are common. Low-growing herbaceous plants, such as grasses and succulents, typically provide less fuel for a fire. Plant fire-resistant ground covers, such as sedums, in bands around buildings or between buildings and large, open spaces to check the advance of rapidly spreading wildfires.

HEAT RELIEF

Where paved surfaces abound, summer heat is more intense. Concrete and asphalt absorb energy from the sun and radiate it back into the atmosphere as heat long after the sun has set. Temperatures may be 15 to 25° F higher in places with lots of paving. Bare soil also stores energy, and radiates heat into the air.

Planting ground covers helps reduce air temperatures (and possibly even air-conditioning costs) in urban areas. Plants transpire, or release water, through pores in their leaves. As this water evaporates into the atmosphere, it cools both the leaf and the environment. The effect of evaporative cooling is most noticeable near large ground cover beds, where temperatures drop 3 or 4° F.

In addition, planting ground covers close to your house or business or along asphalt or concrete walkways and parking lots helps keep you cool by reducing the amount of energy-absorbing surfaces in an area. Ground cover leaves shade soil. By blocking the sun's

energy from reaching the ground, they prevent the soil from absorbing the energy and radiating heat. All plants contribute to evaporative cooling, but ground covers with large leaves, such as hostas or lilies-of-the-valley, have more cooling power, because their larger leaf surfaces shade more area than ground covers with shorter, thinner leaves.

Ground cover plants can improve your immediate environment in other ways. They convert carbon dioxide in the air into oxygen, help filter dust and pollen from the air and pollutants from water flowing past their root systems, and absorb noise. In short, ground covers are workhorses in your landscape.

Ground covers grow in deep shade where turfgrasses and other ornamental plants won't.

This cinquefoil lawn requires little fertilizer, water, or mowing, and it creates a firebreak to protect the house.

DIVAS OF DESIGN

The delightful thing about ground covers is that while they are working so hard, they provide scores of design features such as color and texture, along with seasonal diversity. Without them, many landscapes would look stark or disjointed, certainly plain.

This vibrant mix of ground cover species in a rock garden shows the range of colors and textures found among this group of plants. You also see that they can be used in many ways.

SEASONAL DIVERSITY

Many ground covers change as the seasons progress, adding year-round diversity to a landscape. Their appearance alters as they bud, blossom, and produce fruit, offering ever-shifting colors and textures. Even in winter, when deciduous ground covers lose their leaves, they often reveal rich hues and patterns in their bark. By mixing evergreen ground covers with deciduous ones in your setting, you can enjoy the vitality of growing plants year-round.

COLOR

Ground covers add color to a landscape in a variety of ways. Some have beautifully mottled or variegated leaves in shades of green, yellow, white, or red. Others have lovely blossoms and fruit that add radiant yellows and oranges, delicate pinks and whites, and rich reds and purples to your setting. Some even bring evergreen color to winter landscapes.

Ground covers range in height from 1 inch to 3 feet. This planting of lilyturf, sedum, and ornamental grasses highlights the variety in forms available.

TEXTURE

A solid green landscape can be monotonous, but ground covers—even green-leaved ones—add a visual sense of grain or nap to its beauty. This nap arises from plant texture. Distinctive leaf shapes, sizes, and colors create the texture, as does the ground cover's growth habit. For example, the geometrical leaf shapes and diverse colors of variegated ivies offer textures ranging from coarse to fine.

Plants with shiny, burnished leaves, such as those of European wild ginger, or fuzzy, silvery-gray leaves, such as those of lamb's ear, provide shimmer and depth in the landscape.

By mixing different leaf sizes, textures, and plant forms, you can weave a diverse living fabric into your environment.

GROUND COVER SOLUTIONS

Use ground covers to tie together landscape components. One way to do this is to create a transition from taller elements, such as trees, buildings, and large shrubs, to low-lying turf or walkways by filling the areas between them with plants that are midway in size. Ground covers make this transition gracefully with an assortment of small- to medium-sized plants. For example, pachysandra or plumbago planted beneath a bank of medium-sized shrubs, such as azaleas, allow your eye to flow smoothly along a continuous screen of foliage.

Ground covers camouflage bare spots, such as the shady base of a tree where turfgrasses refuse to spread but lush hostas and ferns will thrive. You can use ground covers to hide unattractive features in your landscape. For example, planting a slope between a building and a flower bed with vinca or jasmine helps hide a barren foundation.

Another use for ground covers is to soften hard edges in a landscape. For example, a veil of Virginia creeper draping over a retaining wall blurs the distinction between the upper and lower levels. Billowy plants such as coral bells create a gentle border along the abrupt margins of walkways and driveways.

Low-growing, traffic-tolerant ground covers, such as thyme, between rocks and pavers visually define a path through taller plants.

Ground covers that cling to nooks and crannies add color and animation to bland, stationary walls or pathways. Sedum and sun rose tucked into the crevices of a rock wall add color and softness and break up the monotony. Irish and Scotch mosses, which tolerate moderate foot traffic, soften the lines between pavers and stepping-stones. Thyme planted in a solid mass along a path adds lushness and releases a delicate aroma when it's crushed underfoot.

Ground covers offer definition to the landscape. As boundaries for flower beds, they establish a natural perimeter around these spaces and visually define the route of a walkway or path. Speedwell, rock rose, or ajuga planted along a path will guide visitors to your front door.

Ground covers provide a foundation for bulbs and annual bedding plants. Sweet woodruff, for example, is a lush green backdrop for bulbs in spring, then it offers its own delicate flowers and fragrance in late spring and into the summer when the bulbs have faded. Vinca provides a year-round background for annual plants.

FOCAL POINTS

Ground covers fill so many familiar functional and design roles that they sometimes seem invisible. But they don't have to be. In fact, they can be the focal point of your yard. Cover a slope with bright pink thrift for drama and appeal. Or plant gazania, with its bright blooms, for a riot of color on a bland site. Cover large areas with ground covers, not small, isolated plantings. For example, ajuga and trailing lantana spread rapidly over large expanses.

Ground covers are versatile and varied, but avoid the temptation to use them so much

that they compete with one another or with other plants rather than complement the setting. A few carefully selected ground covers have greater impact than a hodgepodge of many different types of ground covers.

MOVING AHEAD

Careful planning and selection are the keys to ensuring that ground covers meet your landscaping needs. This book will help. It includes techniques for preparing planting areas and nurturing and maintaining your ground covers. You'll find tips on how to garden more safely and efficiently. And, at the end of the book, a Plant Selection Guide provides detailed information on common ground cover plants that fit your growing conditions and gardening goals.

In this setting, ground covers provide the low-growing, unifying element that ties together trees, shrubs, pavers, and lawn areas.

SELECTING GROUND COVERS

As part of the planning process, identify areas where ground covers can help, either by solving a problem or by filling a design role—or both, like this planting of lavender cotton and white rock rose, which stabilizes the slope and beautifies it.

Now that you know the potential of ground covers in a landscape, it's time to figure out where they can go to work for you. Then you can make decisions as to which ground covers match the design and functional requirements of your particular landscape.

PLANNING

First, you must know why and how you want to use ground covers. What short- and long-range goals will these versatile plants help you meet? Begin by visualizing the big picture of your entire landscape.

Walk into your yard and look around. Get a visual image of your existing landscape. Yes, you already know what's there. But take the time to really see your yard.

Identify its permanent elements, such as trees, concrete walkways, outbuildings, the swimming pool, the water garden, fences, flower beds or rock gardens, and other components that you plan to keep. Next, identify problem areas and any elements that you dislike about the landscape, such as patches of bare ground or barren sections of retaining walls, steep slopes that are difficult to mow or are eroding, gaps between existing plants and your lawn, shady spots under trees,

Runoff, even on gentle slopes, can wash away nonliving ground covers, such as this mulch, and make your landscape look bare and shabby. Living ground covers planted in these areas will hold the soil in place while also beautifying the bare ground.

wet or dry spots where nothing seems to grow, unsightly areas around drains or culverts, weedy or unkempt areas, or simply spots where the landscape seems drab or disjointed.

Also, note the cause of the problem areas. For example, is an area too wet, dry, or shady? Does the current design no longer suit your taste? Have you added new structures since the original landscape was established, leaving the area looking fragmented or, perhaps, creating new problems by redirecting runoff and forming a wet spot or by deepening shade so nothing will grow?

Finally, think about the future. Do your plans include installing a new structure such as a pool, storage shed, or playhouse that won't fit in with the current landscape design?

As you examine the big picture, think about where ground covers might help. Ground covers are better solutions for some problems than for others. Look for places that call out for low-growing plants, such as bare, shady spots under shrubs and trees, areas of rough or sloping terrain where mowing and maintenance are difficult, or parts of the landscape that would be beautiful carpeted with lush, low-growing plants.

CAPTURING THE PLAN

With this big picture in mind, you can hire a professional landscaper to create a design, or you can develop a plan yourself with surprising (and rewarding) ease. Here's how.

Photograph your current landscape, either in one large panoramic shot or in several smaller shots that you can tape together to form a panorama. These "before" photos help document changes. They'll help especially if you need advice from a professional when selecting plant material.

Shallow tree roots break up the smooth look of a lawn and are difficult to mow around. Ground covers hide roots by trailing across them.

Deeply shaded areas beneath trees will rarely support a lawn, but shade-tolerant ground covers thrive.

PLANNING
continued

Drawing your landscape plan using correct measurements and a plot plan is the first step in developing a landscape design that makes the best use of ground covers and all your plants.

Take the photos with you to the nursery or garden center so the sales staff can better understand your needs.

MAP YOUR LANDSCAPE

Next, make a base map of your current landscape. This is simply a diagram or illustration of the yard that forms the basis for all your plans. It will help you think through your plant selection and placement options before you invest time and money in changes that may not work. And it lets you connect ground cover selection to the big picture so that the various components of your landscape flow together beautifully.

Without a plan, you might be tempted to simply plop plants into problem areas without much forethought, perhaps magnifying existing problems or creating new ones. If plants aren't suited for the location, they

can be difficult to maintain and may even die. Or they may make the landscape look disjointed and haphazard because they don't fit the overall design.

You don't have to be artistic with your plot plan; a simple sketch will do. However, you will need accurate dimensions of the bed area to order the right number of plants, so measure your yard, then draw the base map to scale. It will help to have someone hold one end of a long tape measure while you take measurements.

Transfer these dimensions to graph paper (1 inch equals 10 feet), noting north and south on the drawing and indicating all property lines and angles. Include easement measurements from city records. Then draw in all existing buildings and paved areas, such as driveways, sidewalks, and walkways.

Once you've drawn the base map, sketch in any large permanent plantings or structures that you plan to keep—trees, hedges, and flower beds, for example.

EXPERIMENTING

Now you're ready to incorporate your ideas. Lay tracing paper over the plot plan. Sketch out any and all thoughts you have about changing your current landscape. For example, if you want to enlarge a bed or replace some lawn with ground covers, sketch new borders on the tracing paper to see how your ideas will fit.

It may take several trial sketches to find one that suits your tastes, so keep experimenting until you're happy with the outcome. And remember, there's no one correct design for a yard. View these sketches as a chance to brainstorm ideas. Avoid censuring your ideas; one off-the-wall design

If you need help visualizing your landscape in three dimensions, build a tabletop model using household items to represent structures. Delineate ground cover beds and walkways with string.

Another way to try out a plan is to "plant" it with items such as trash cans, laundry baskets, empty pots, and hoses. These items can be easily moved around to achieve the desired effect and give you an idea of how the actual plants will look.

may lead you to the perfect solution for your landscape.

THREE-DIMENSIONAL PLANS

If you can't visualize how your plan will translate to the yard, you can bring this two-dimensional image to life by arranging a tabletop model. You'll need at least two colors of string or yarn, tape, and a few handy household items to represent existing structures and plants, such as a magazine or sheet of paper to signify your house, small notepads to denote outbuildings or other structures, and glasses, salt shakers, bottles, and similar small objects to represent trees and shrubs. Try to find objects with shapes similar to those of the plants in your yard.

Arrange these objects on the table in their existing locations in your landscape. Then mark existing walkways, driveways, flower beds, and other physical boundaries with one color of string or yarn. Tape this string in place so it won't shift as you work.

Next, outline the boundaries for ground cover areas with the other colored string. This is your "play" string; use it to experiment with as many arrangements as you can come up with. As you tinker with it, think about new elements you hope to add to your landscape. Do you plan to establish a new, colorful flower bed to liven up a drab spot or soften a stark area? Do you want to remove existing plants and start a new bed from scratch? You may want to use a third color of string to outline all the other ideas you have.

When you are satisfied with the design, secure the string to the table with tape.

Photograph your tabletop scene so you can retain the image for future reference and put away the household items.

This tabletop model is only a guide to your landscaping plans, not a blueprint that's set in stone. It's quite all right to change the design as you begin the actual work.

PRIORITIZING

Set priorities for your projects based on your list of problems and your visual images of the landscape. Renovating a landscape takes time, money, and energy, and it must often be done in stages based on your time and resources.

If, for example, your renovations require moving soil to install a drainage system or irrigation lines or to build retaining walls, start with these projects, then undertake cosmetic changes and repairs. By tackling projects in this order, you avoid damaging earlier projects and having to redo them.

List your projects in order of importance, and think again about how ground covers fit in. There may be spots where they are part of the overall landscaping plan—perhaps to fill in under new shrubs. In other places, ground covers may be the focus of your desired changes. Decide where and how you want to use ground covers, and plan your purchases accordingly.

Finally, be sure to file the information—lists, drawings, and photographs—for future reference. Even if you finish the landscape in one season, you won't regret having the information on hand if you decide to make more changes later.

GROUND COVERS FOR THE SITE

Match ground covers to the microclimate. Where the microclimate creates an environment much different from normal, take advantage of it.

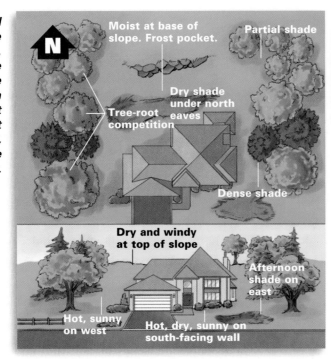

Moist at base of slope. Frost pocket.

Partial shade

Dry shade under north eaves

Tree-root competition

Dense shade

Dry and windy at top of slope

Afternoon shade on east

Hot, sunny on west

Hot, dry, sunny on south-facing wall

Moist at base of slope, dry on top

Having a base plan will help you decide which plant qualities best meet the needs of your landscape. The next step is to identify the growing conditions in your yard, then find plants that thrive under those conditions.

GROUND COVERS FOR FULL SUN

Artemisia
Broom
Cotoneaster
Coyote brush
Creeping manzanita
Dwarf rosemary
Fleabane
Juniper
Lavender
Lippia
Moss phlox
Rock rose
Rose
Sedum
Snow-in-summer
Sun rose
Trailing lantana
Woolly yarrow

HARDINESS ZONES

Some plants thrive only in certain climates, while others grow virtually anywhere. For most plants, though, cold temperatures are *the* limiting environmental factor. Although some plants readily tolerate –20° F, others quickly succumb when the temperature drops to only 10° F. So the first thing to look for in a ground cover is hardiness.

Plant hardiness zones identify the coldest temperatures expected in a region. The map on page 96 will help you determine the hardiness zone of your locality. Then, as you browse the Plant Selection Guide, which starts on page 52, you'll notice that each entry specifies a hardiness zone. Any ground cover with a hardiness rating that matches the climate in your region, or that can take colder weather, should do fine in your yard. For example, if you live in Zone 6, you can grow plants that are hardy in Zones 4 to 6, but not plants hardy only to Zone 7.

MICROCLIMATES

Microclimates can put a kink into this broad statement of hardiness. These are small areas where the soil and climate differ from surrounding areas. Often they are affected by the contour of your terrain. For example, cold air has a tendency to slide down a hill and accumulate at the bottom. So the bottom of a hill and other low-lying areas may be more prone to frost than the rest of your yard. In fact, this area may be cold enough that you need to plant a ground cover that is a zone hardier. Water also runs down slopes, and the bases of slopes are usually wet. At the same time, the tops of hills and slopes may be drier than other areas; select drought-tolerant plants for these spots.

Exposures also affect soil and air temperatures. Typically, a southern exposure warms the landscape; areas facing north tend to be colder.

Areas next to the house are generally warmer than outlying areas. Here you might be able to plant a Zone 7 ground cover in your Zone 6 landscape. Soil next to a building with a concrete foundation may be more alkaline, too, and runoff from your roof or gutters can keep these areas damp. And you should be aware that drying wind tunnels can occur between houses.

You can identify the microclimates in your landscape by observing existing plants. Plants may seem lusher and more productive in some spots while only certain plants may flourish in others. Discrepancies in plant growth are signs that growing conditions are not the same on every site.

SOIL TYPES

If your landscape is endowed with rich, fertile soil, nearly any ground cover plant will thrive. If, however, your soil is less than ideal, don't despair. There is a ground cover for virtually any site.

For example, plants such as rosemary, cotoneaster, phlox, and germander require few nutrients and grow in poor soil. For dry sites, succulents and other drought-tolerant plants, such as lantana, ice plants, or grapeholly, are available. Wet soil is ideal for bog plants such as moneywort, many ferns, and ribbon grass.

Sun and shade also affect your choices. For a wooded area, choose shade-tolerant plants, such as ferns, hostas, and vinca. Use sun-loving plants, such as snow-in-summer, yarrow, or broom, on sunny sites.

SEVERE ENVIRONMENTS

Because ground covers tend to be hardy and versatile, many are well-adapted to severe climates where few other plants will grow, even in regions with extreme environmental conditions.

Near a coastline with salty air and soil and windy skies, select ground covers that withstand salinity and drier, breezier conditions. Among these are manzanita, kew broom, heaths, and shrubby veronica. In a desert region, you'll want drought-tolerant plants that can take alkaline soils, such as some ice plants, lantana, gazania, yarrow, and coyote brush.

The quick-reference tables at right offer a sampling of plants for specific sites. The Plant Selection Guide details site needs for other ground covers.

GROUND COVERS FOR DRY SITES

Cotoneaster
Gazania
Grapeholly
Juniper
Ice plant (some species)
Rosemary
St. Johnswort
Trailing lantana
Yarrow

Dry, sunny spots next to pavement call for tough plants, such as blue fescue.

GROUND COVERS FOR WET SITES

Chinese astilbe   Lilyturf
Ferns   Moneywort
Forget-me-not   Ribbon grass
Hostas   Yellow-root

Forget-me-nots (background) are a good choice for wet, boggy soil.

GROUND COVERS FOR DEEP SHADE

Barrenwort   Lily-of-the-
Bunchberry   valley
Cast-iron plant   Pachysandra
English ivy   Sweet woodruff
Ferns   Wandflower
Hostas   Wild ginger

GROUND COVERS FOR TRAFFIC

Blue star   Lippia
  creeper   Mock
Chamomile   strawberry
Creeping   New Zealand
  speedwell   brass buttons
Irish moss   Thyme

GROUND COVERS FOR DESERT REGIONS

In desert settings, plant drought-resistant ground cover plants such as lavender cotton and junipers.

Bush morning
  glory
Dwarf coyote
  brush
Gazania
Manzanita
Mother-of-
  thyme
Rosemary
Snow-in-
  summer
Trailing indigo
  bush

GROUND COVERS FOR THE SEASIDE

Broom   Manzanita
Ice plants   Speedwell
Lantana   Wedelia

FUNCTION AND DESIGN

Design roles include bridging the transition between use areas and softening hardscapes. Here, the best ground cover for those roles must also take foot traffic.

Vinca offers many of the characteristics necessary for it to serve as a low-maintenance lawn substitute. It is a low-growing evergreen that forms a dense cover and withstands some traffic.

Mesh function and design into your selection of ground cover plants, because function and design are dictated by a plant's type. Woody plants give permanence to a landscape, while herbaceous plants offer a lush, carpeted impression only during the growing season. Evergreen plants bring year-round color and structure to a landscape; deciduous plants lose their leaves in winter, which may reveal different stem colors or add new textures to the landscape. Or they may simply seem to disappear.

You can mix and match these different qualities—woody, herbaceous, evergreen, and deciduous; the options are almost endless. But to fully understand the options, you must understand the language, both in a functional sense and in a design sense.

HERBACEOUS OR WOODY?

Plants are described as either herbaceous or woody. Both types make fine ground covers; however, each brings a different element to the landscape and fills different roles.

HERBACEOUS GROUND COVERS: Herbaceous plants have little or no woody tissue. Their stems are fleshy and supple rather than rigid, and aboveground portions tend to be leaflike in structure and texture. Herbaceous ground covers grow in a wide range of shapes, sizes, and colors. For example, lilyturf provides height and grassy shape and texture; ajuga and vinca create a low carpet; lavender cotton forms a silvery ball of foliage.

Perennial herbaceous plants die back to the ground each winter, then produce new shoots and leaves each spring, which is how they cope with cold. For that reason, they don't provide the same year-round visual structure as woody plants. But they are lush during the growing season and often have showier flowers, foliage, and seeds than woody ground covers. They also supply seasonal diversity to your setting as they grow, bloom, and later die back.

Most herbaceous ground covers have fibrous roots and dense growth, which helps stabilize soil and prevents erosion.

Although herbaceous plants may be annual (living only one year), biennial (two years), or perennial (more than two years), this book focuses on herbaceous perennials because they seldom have to be replaced.

WOODY GROUND COVERS: Woody plants include trees, shrubs, and many shrubby ground covers such as junipers, cotoneasters, barberries, and vines.

Unlike herbaceous plants, woody plant cells contain lignin, a cellulose fiber that produces rigid rather than pliable stems and limbs. For that reason, woody plants maintain their form year-round. Even without their leaves, deciduous woody ground covers form lovely silhouettes in the landscape.

There are no set rules about when and where to use woody ground covers instead of herbaceous ground covers, but they're ideal for spots requiring a year-round presence, such as where boundary plants are called for. Woody ground covers can be superb boundary plants because, when placed close together, they provide a solid, year-round barrier.

A SAMPLING OF HERBACEOUS GROUND COVERS

Cinquefoil	Moneywort
Goutweed	Vinca
Hostas	Wild strawberry
Lily-of-the-valley	Yellow archangel

For example, the thorns and height of ground cover barberries prevent people walking in certain areas, even when snow covers them.

Because the stems of most woody ground covers don't form roots wherever their branches touch the ground, they don't prevent erosion until their canopies completely cover the ground. Once that happens and their root systems fill the soil, they do a good job of holding the soil.

DECIDUOUS OR EVERGREEN?

Like all plants, ground covers can be deciduous or evergreen. Both types fill design and functional roles in landscapes.

Deciduous plants lose their leaves in fall and are bare in winter. Evergreens retain their foliage, staying green and functional year-round. However, they tend to be less colorful and seasonally diverse than deciduous plants.

Some plant groups have deciduous and evergreen members. For example, creeping cotoneaster is deciduous, while bearberry cotoneaster is evergreen. Other plants are deciduous or evergreen depending on climatic conditions. For example, in warm areas, New Zealand brass buttons tend to be evergreen, but in cold climates, it is deciduous. Check the Plant Selection Guide to ensure you select a true evergreen if that is what your landscape requires.

WHICH IS BEST?

The best option often is to mix evergreen and deciduous plants in a landscape. In certain spots, consistent, year-round foliage may be more important than color and diversity. For example, evergreen ground covers work best in year-round roles, such as directing foot traffic through your landscape to the front door or creating design structure in the front yard. Color and diversity tend to be more important in accent roles.

Intersperse plantings of evergreen and deciduous plants where you want the best of both plant types. To ensure success, select species with compatible growth habits and cultural needs.

PLANTS FOR SPECIAL EFFECTS

Some ground covers, such as vines, ferns, mosses, and ornamental grasses, readily fill special landscaping needs.

VINES: Vines make excellent ground covers. They ramble and tumble more than other types of plants and fit niches that few other plants can. Because they can be used both vertically and horizontally to cover a wide range of areas, from slopes and gullies to rock,

Woody plants, even deciduous species, have a year-round presence in the landscape. They make good boundary or barrier plants.

concrete, or brick walls, vines are particularly effective at softening hard edges. And some, such as ivy, provide soil-holding benefits as well, because they develop roots along their stems as they grow.

Vines grow by either twining or clinging. Clinging vines, such as creeping fig, Virginia creeper, and English ivy, can crawl up a solid wall, structure, or tree trunk as well as lie flat on the ground. Twining vines, such as clematis, require something to hang on to and twist around as they climb. They do better draped over a solid wall. Avoid aggressive twining vines, such as Japanese honeysuckle, which grow by wrapping themselves around an object. They can overtake their neighbors, strangling or smothering them.

FERNS: Ferns can be intriguingly ornamental while filling a functional role. They have a wide range of charming leaf structures, such as the fuzzy, delicate fronds of maidenhair ferns or the larger and more defined fronds of shield ferns. Some, such as Japanese painted fern, have colorfully tinged fronds.

Because most ferns prefer shady, moist areas, you can plant them where lawn and other more traditional ground covers won't grow. Native ferns are more hardy

A FEW WOODY GROUND COVERS

Barberry	Coyote brush	Rose
Broom	Indigo	Russian cypress
Bush honeysuckle	Ivy	Virginia creeper
Cotoneaster	Juniper	Wintergreen

FUNCTION AND DESIGN
continued

Ferns, such as this ostrich fern, add height, texture, and color to shady areas.

Vines, such as this star jasmine, trail across bare ground or cascade over walls, providing a graceful touch to the landscape.

and versatile than exotic or imported ferns.

MOSSES: Mosses are a lush and enchanting ground cover option. Although they are sometimes difficult to establish and slow to spread, once they take hold they are practically maintenance-free and resilient to foot traffic. Use mosses where the soil is poor and between stepping-stones and rocks. Star, fern, broom, cedar, and hairy-cap mosses grow in almost any climate.

GRASSES: Ornamental grasses bring subtle color and texture to a ground cover bed. They are lovely as edging plants and spread well to fill large areas. Grasses often have a longer growing season than other herbaceous perennials. Although their foliage dies back in winter, you can leave it in place to provide a winter presence. In addition, most have lovely seed heads to dress up a winter landscape. Some ornamental grasses, such as blue fescue, grow in clumps rather than spreading to form a solid mat of plants.

For more help on selecting a ground cover, refer to the Plant Selection Guide, which offers information on the cultural needs of a

wide range of ground covers. Leaf through the pages and get a feel for the plants that fit your needs and tastes. Ask experienced local gardeners or nursery staff about the plants that work well in your area. You may also want to experiment with unfamiliar ground cover plants. Establish a small test planting before using them in large quantities.

Grassy blue fescue's color creates a subtle backdrop for other plants.

GROUND COVERS FOR THE JOB

Role	Plant Characteristics	Examples
Erosion control	Perennials with fibrous root systems that spread quickly to cover the soil and have foliage during the rainy seasons; or woody evergreens, which retain their leaves year-round	Grasses, daylily, juniper, cotoneaster, ajuga, honeysuckle
Directing foot traffic or forming a barrier	Taller ground covers (1½ to 2 feet high); woody plants that offer more structure or have thorns	Lilyturf, barberry, heavenly bamboo, rosemary, juniper
Firebreak	Plants with fleshy, moisture-retaining foliage and small leaves	Dwarf coyote brush, rock rose, African daisy, sedum, artemisia, ice plant
Softening edges of walkways, driveways	Low to moderate-height plants that add a soft texture to the landscape	Dwarf plumbago, goutweed, bergenia, pinks, baby's breath, wall germander, barrenworts
Lawn substitute	Low-growing, matting or widely spreading herbaceous plants that withstand at least some foot traffic; plants with year-round presence	Chamomile, New Zealand brass buttons, sandwort, ornamental grasses, lilyturf, lippia, vinca
Woodland and natural settings	Plants of moderate height that add color, variety, and texture	Wild ginger, bunchberry, fern, hosta, sweet woodruff, barrenwort
Foundation plantings	Shrubs and taller plants that form a solid visual cover to hide foundations	Cotoneaster, ivy, juniper, star jasmine, Russian cypress
Between stepping-stones	Low-growing plants that tolerate some foot traffic	Thyme, moneywort, speedwell, chamomile, thrift, sedum, lippia, moneywort
Covering walls	Trailing or climbing plants, or plants that cling to cracks and crevices in rock walls	Ivy, jasmine, rose, sedum

ALTERNATIVE GROUND COVERS

The broad definition of ground covers encompasses nonliving materials as well as plants. It includes organic materials, such as wood, bark chips, and cocoa hulls, and inorganic materials, such as rock, pebbles, gravel, and pavers.

These materials help stabilize soil, discourage weeds, and present a low, massed appearance. More importantly, they contribute unique design qualities to a landscape.

Typically, most people think of nonliving materials as surfaces only for paths, patios, or other hardscaping or for mulching. And it's no wonder, after the bashing homeowners and landscapers took for using decorative white rock mulches in the 1970s.

However, nonliving materials offer as much design potential in a landscape as ground cover plants. The design effects they create are quite different from those of ground cover plants but are just as beautiful. Like plants, they add texture—from fine to coarse—and color—generally neutral shades of tan or brown, but also black and other colors. Use nonliving ground covers to create a swath of color through a landscape, to draw a pattern, to add textural or color contrast between plants and hardscapes, or as substitutes for lawn.

LIVING OR NONLIVING?

Consider both function and design when deciding whether you want a living or nonliving ground cover in your landscape.

Nonliving ground covers help unify the design of the landscape, just like plants. Some materials, such as pavers, also allow you to use the area in different ways from ground covers and lawn. Because their colors are so different from those of plants, nonliving ground covers are particularly effective at drawing attention to a spot in a landscape. They can also direct traffic. Rather than blocking entrance, however, they provide access.

The textures of nonliving ground covers tend to be finer than those of most ground cover plants, so they blend and contrast well with plants. In addition, because they are lower to the ground, they enhance the transition between planting areas.

Nonliving ground covers are ideal in small spots where ground cover plants might crowd the bed or where they would compete with shrubs and other landscape plants for water and nutrients. They make especially effective textural accents in small spaces.

They do well in heavy-traffic areas, such as footpaths, where living plants may not survive. For example, square stepping-stones surrounded by the same color gravel instead of plants provide a sturdy yet interesting walk.

In areas prone to erosion, nonliving materials are not the best choice. Although they prevent rain and irrigation water from breaking up soil surfaces, they are only surface treatments. They don't stop soil on slopes from becoming saturated; the soil can still slide down a hill in a heavy rain. Also, bark is lightweight, floating in water even on flat land.

Weeds can grow among nonliving ground covers just as they do among plants. It's much simpler, though, to apply a nonselective herbicide cover spray over these materials than over plants or to mow down the weeds.

MINERAL OR ORGANIC?

Cost is one factor to consider. Rocks, gravel, and other inorganic materials may cost more than some organic mulches, but usually, they

Is it a patio or an area of nonliving ground cover? It's both. The combination of chamomile and pavers would be interesting, even without patio furniture to suggest a traditional use.

Nonliving ground covers add texture, color, and pattern and require no care.

ALTERNATIVE GROUND COVERS
continued

represent a one-time investment, which makes them cheaper over the long term. Organic materials, even though less expensive initially, end up costing more as you regularly replenish them.

Inorganic ground covers heat the atmosphere more than organic ones do. They absorb heat during the day, then radiate it back to the atmosphere at night.

Areas close to your house may be better suited for mineral ground covers. These areas can be breeding grounds for pests that might invade your home. For example, some insects, such as smoky brown cockroaches, millipedes, earwigs, spiders, and box elder bugs, spend most of their lives outdoors but venture into the house for visits, especially as the weather cools in autumn.

These pests, known as peridomestic insects, thrive in the damp, dark environments provided by organic and living ground covers. Organic and living ground covers under the eaves of your home may encourage the insects to set up housekeeping just outside your door, close enough to enter easily. In areas close to

homes and office buildings, consider using materials that provide good drainage and don't hold water, such as gravel and rocks.

Mineral ground covers offer one big advantage over organic and living ground covers. They don't have to be fertilized or watered and they typically don't need to be replaced, only periodically refreshed. But they also don't fortify the soil. Organic ground covers, on the other hand, enrich the soil, although, in turn, they require additional labor to maintain because they break down eventually and have to be replenished.

KEY TO SUCCESS

Consider the Japanese Zen garden with its raked gravel when deciding how to use nonliving ground covers. Notice that these gardens incorporate materials in colors that complement rather than contrast highly with other elements in the landscape. And they use earthy colors that seem to blend in naturally. In your garden, try brown-tinted river rock with landscape timbers or black cobblestones with slate pavers. Save highly contrasting materials to use as small accents.

When selecting alternative ground covers, consider their aesthetic qualities. Note how these three ground covers vary in texture and color. Each will bring a different look, style, and mood to your landscape. For example, river rock is much less formal than brick, and bark chips fade into the background.

TURFGRASS, OR NOT TURFGRASS?

Turfgrass is the best ground cover for playgrounds and other areas that receive a lot of foot traffic. It is resilient and safe.

Turfgrasses are the best-known and most commonly used ground covers. However, they are not always the best choice for all situations.

PROS AND CONS

Expanses of yard where ample sunlight is available and people walk or play are ideal for turf. A healthy lawn has tremendous cushioning ability, which makes it one of the safest places for children to play.

The smooth surface of a lawn provides a tidy foreground that accentuates other areas of the landscape and gives it an open feeling. Bands or ribbons of turf form beautiful pathways through a garden, blending gracefully into ornamental plantings.

However, turf has its drawbacks. Most lawns have to be mowed (at least weekly for half the year), fertilized, and watered regularly to maintain their health and beauty. And like all plants, turfgrasses are susceptible to diseases and pests. Yes, other plant ground covers require regular care, but usually you can get by with only an occasional grooming.

Turfgrasses are among the best plants for holding a slope in place. However, mowing a steep slope is one of the few truly dangerous activities in a landscape. Since safety shutoffs have become standard on mowers, it's less likely that you'll lose a limb when mowing slopes, but you can break bones if you fall.

Few turfgrass species withstand extremely shady areas, which is one reason bare spots develop underneath trees and shrubs. And only a handful of turfgrass species are available, while hundreds of other ground cover options exist.

NEW BEGINNINGS

If you're starting a landscape from scratch, decide in advance just how much space you really need for lawn.

First, consider how your family will use the yard. You may want small areas for a picnic table and casual outdoor seating, or you may need larger expanses for the kids to play. Its flat, even surface makes turf best for these uses. Also, plant it in heavily trafficked areas. Then think about how alternative ground covers—other plants, pavers, rocks, gravel, or bark chips—can complete the design of your landscape.

In existing yards, look for problem areas: "cow paths," bare spots under trees, anyplace the lawn is not thriving. These areas offer the opportunity to plant ground covers. Match your selection to the growing conditions in the area. And take time to consider design options. Rather than simply concentrating on the problem spot, think about how to use ground covers to bring swaths of contrasting color and texture to your landscape.

GROWING GROUND COVERS

Take time to plan and properly plant your ground covers so they will have a good start in life.

There's more to establishing ground covers than plunking plants into the dirt. Investing time and resources in the planting and early care of a ground cover bed will pay off later with easier maintenance and thriving plants.

Among the steps to success is taking extra pains until the plants are "established." A plant is established when it grows and thrives with little extra watering and no longer depends on you for survival. Being established doesn't mean the plant stops growing; it means its roots, stems, and crown are self-sufficient.

Most herbaceous plants are established within a month or two. Woody plants may take several months. Plants are not yet established if they wilt at midday. When they can go a week or more without water under normal conditions, they are established.

An established ground cover bed is different. A bed is established when each plant has rooted well and the foliage covers the area.

Established beds require little or no weeding and only moderate watering; they grow well and, if they flower, bloom abundantly. It may take one to three years for a bed to fully establish, depending on spacing, types of plants, and growing conditions in the bed.

STEPS TO ESTABLISHMENT

Establishment starts with site preparation. Besides amending the soil so that it offers a fertile, weed-free home for the plants, site preparation involves laying out the planting design to make installation easier and ensure good coverage as the bed matures.

Next is buying plants and selecting the healthiest specimens. Once planted, attentive maintenance helps plants settle in and sustains them through the years.

Read on for information on how to do all this and more, such as helpful hints that will make your gardening efforts easier.

PREPARING TO PLANT

Planting ground covers requires planning and forethought. You'll need to establish the bed's borders, eliminate weeds and unwanted plants so they won't compete with your new ground covers, prepare the soil to make it as fertile and productive as possible, and level the soil so it provides an attractive, even surface for planting.

ESTABLISHING BORDERS

Use a hose to mark the boundaries of the ground cover bed. Hoses are usually long enough to mark a bed, and they are lightweight and flexible so they are easy to move around until you're satisfied with the size and shape of the bed. Once you are happy, mark the bed's outline with powdered chalk, ground limestone, sand, or spray paint. Then you can put away the hose.

CLEARING THE SITE

Now it's time to get your hands in the dirt. First, remove any unwanted plants—ornamentals, sod, and weeds—that might compete with the ground covers as they're becoming established.

It's almost impossible to eliminate weeds from a site, but controlling them before planting will reduce the scope of future outbreaks. You have three options for eliminating weeds: applying herbicides, using mechanical methods such as tilling and hoeing, and employing physical methods such as mulching or solarizing the soil.

You may prefer a totally organic approach, especially in an area where it's hard to spray herbicides without damaging neighboring plants. But if you are working in a large space where other methods are not practical, consider using herbicides. They offer the fastest, least labor-intensive option. Some weeds are so pernicious and well-established that the only way to control them is with herbicides. Often, combining methods—for example, spraying an area, then hoeing seedlings that crop up later—is an efficient, low-impact method of eliminating weeds.

CHEMICAL METHODS: Herbicides take several forms. Nonselective herbicides, such as glyphosate or diquat dibromide, kill almost any plant at any stage of growth. Selective herbicides work on specific plants. For example, triclopyr kills woody plants such as vines and shrubs; fluazifop kills grasses. Postemergence herbicides are effective against weeds that have emerged and are past the seedling stage. Preemergence herbicides inhibit seed germination; some kill seedlings. Contact herbicides kill only the plant parts that come in direct contact with the chemical. Translocated herbicides are absorbed by the plant's leaves and stems and carried to the roots, killing the whole plant.

Nursery personnel can help you select the correct herbicide for your needs. Explain to them which plants you are trying to remove, the proximity of other plantings, and other site factors that may help determine which product is appropriate.

Besides selecting an herbicide that targets your weed problem, be aware that careful handling and application of chemicals is the key to success. Read the product label carefully to ensure that you are using the herbicide properly and safely. Don't use herbicides on windy days, when breezes might blow them onto other plants, or in extremely hot weather, when they may vaporize and affect desirable plants. If you must use an herbicide near existing plants, cover the desirable plants with plastic to protect them from chemical drift.

Contact your local extension office if you have any questions about selecting an herbicide or using it correctly.

PHYSICAL METHODS: Employ physical methods if you are establishing ground covers in a bed around existing plants. In this situation, extensive hoeing and tilling may damage the roots of existing plants, and chemicals may be too risky. Mulching will help control weeds as your ground covers become established. One method is to smother weeds by mulching the area with newspapers or black plastic about two weeks before planting ground covers.

A more effective method is solarization, which uses high temperatures to kill weeds, weed seeds, microorganisms (it doesn't discriminate between disease and beneficial

The first step in establishing ground covers is to clear away all vegetation from the area. Turfgrass can often be lifted and used elsewhere in the landscape.

PREPARING TO PLANT
continued

microbes), and other soil pests. It works best during hot, sunny periods.

To solarize soil, clear the area of rocks, debris, and weeds. Wet the soil thoroughly, then lay 1- to 4-mil clear plastic on the soil surface. Because solarization could harm the roots of nearby plants, lay the plastic only up

Once the majority of the existing vegetation is cleared away, you may need to hoe the area to remove deeply rooted weeds.

to their drip lines. Set weighted cans or bricks on the plastic—throughout the entire area, not just the perimeter—then lay a second layer of plastic over them. This creates an airspace that helps to heat the soil. Secure the edges of the plastic with soil, rocks, or boards to seal the cover. Leave the plastic in place for four to eight weeks.

MECHANICAL METHODS: Mechanical methods are ideal for small areas but may be too backbreaking when preparing a large area. Hoeing to a depth of 1 to 2 inches removes most shallow-rooted weeds. Tackle hand-weeding after a rain, or moisten the soil with a sprinkler a day or so before going to work; it's easier to pull roots out of damp soil than out of dry soil.

For large sites, use a rototiller to clear the bed. Excessive tilling, however, breaks down the soil structure, making it erosion-prone, and can cause a hard, impenetrable layer to form under the top layer of soil. If you use a rototiller, avoid tilling when soil is wet, make only one or two passes and incorporate organic matter into the soil at the same time you till it.

Deeper-rooted species, such as dandelions, may require hand-weeding or deep cultivation to remove their entire root systems as well as

any rhizomes and stolons. Be aware that dandelions, plants that spread by stolons or rhizomes, such as bermudagrass, and many other tough weeds readily regenerate new plants from any tiny bit of root left in the soil. Tilling especially helps these weeds spread. You'll need to balance the amount of time you have available with the effort it will take to rid the planting area of these species when you select a control method.

After hoeing or hand-weeding, remove the dislodged weeds from the bed. If they're mainly annual weeds, you can leave them on the bed to wither and die and add organic matter to the soil. However, if you leave them there, don't irrigate the area for several days to ensure that the weeds won't sprout back to life. If the weeds have already formed seeds, throw them away to prevent new infestations.

No matter which method you use to clear the bed, once it is clean, water it well and wait a week to see if new weeds emerge. If only a few pop up, remove them and begin the next step of bed preparation. If new weeds quickly crowd the area, repeat the process until no more weeds emerge.

REMOVING SOD

If sod in the planting area is tightly knit and not too deeply rooted, you can remove it intact and use it in other parts of your yard. Sod is easily removed with a sod cutter, which you can rent. Or you can dig up the sod by hand. Removing sod works much better if the soil is moist, so wait until after a rain, or water a few days before you tackle the task.

With a spade, score the sod into 1- to 2-foot-wide strips. Starting at the outside edge of the bed, dig under the roots with the spade, lifting up with its tip to loosen the roots from the soil. Pull back on the sod to lift it. This may take two people, one to dig and one to pull at the same time. Continue cutting the strip, using short jabbing and lifting strokes of the spade. Often, once you have loosened the sod, you can roll it up with relative ease. A final shallow hoeing will eliminate many of the remaining sod or weed roots in the bed.

In some instances, you may want to plant directly into sod rather than clear the site. This is advisable under certain conditions, such as where tilling or hoeing will disturb existing plants, bulbs, or roots of nearby trees or shrubs, or on sites that are difficult to work or prone to erosion. If the sod is left in place, its roots can hold the slope until the ground cover becomes established.

Plant through the sod if the soil quality underneath is satisfactory (the soil is not compacted and is high in organic matter). Kill the sod with a nonselective herbicide, such as glyphosate, wait 10 days, then dig through the dead sod to plant.

GOOD SOIL

After clearing the planting beds, turn your attention to your soil's quality. The best soils are loamy. Not every landscape, however, is blessed with ideal soil. You can improve soil quality by adding organic matter (such as compost and manure), lime or sulfur, sand, or fertilizer before planting.

Soil is a mixture of mineral particles, organic matter, air, and water. Two layers of soil are of primary concern to gardeners: topsoil, which is the layer closest to the surface, and subsoil, which is the layer immediately below the topsoil.

TOPSOIL: Most plant roots reside in the topsoil layer, so this is where the most organic matter and fertility are needed. Topsoil should be porous and loose enough for water—along with the nutrients it carries—and air to move through and for roots to grow. Ideally, topsoil should be 18 to 20 inches deep, but in many regions, erosion has reduced this layer. Dry, desert regions have shallow topsoil because the lack of moisture slows its formation.

If your topsoil is shallow, buy enough replacement soil to cover the entire bed 4 to 6 inches deep and spread it over the area. The soil should have the same texture or be lighter in texture than existing soil. This ensures that water easily infiltrates and drains through the soil. You may have to inspect the topsoil yourself to make sure it is all right. Check that it is a relatively dark color and not too sticky (clay soil) or sandy. Ask local nurseries or fellow gardeners about reputable sources of high-quality topsoil.

Soil blends are also available, though they typically are more expensive than standard topsoil. Blends, sometimes known as "improved soil," have been amended with organic matter. Because blends are expensive, they are usually most feasible for small beds.

SUBSOIL: The subsoil layer is naturally more compact and dense than topsoil. It is composed of minerals that have not yet weathered into topsoil. If this layer is very dense or compacted, it affects plant health by restricting water flow and root growth.

Traffic on the soil surface or excessive tilling can cause an impenetrable mantle known as a plow layer (also called hardpan) to form in the soil. If you encounter a hard, impenetrable layer as you prepare the beds, you have hit a plow layer. A plow pan can hinder healthy plant growth.

Dig through hardpan with a pickax, jackhammer, or posthole digger until you reach a softer layer underneath. Stagger the

Good soil is dark in color with a crumbly texture. You should be able to squeeze damp soil in the palm of your hand so it forms a ball that readily crumbles when you release it.

holes about 2 feet apart to allow drainage. Refill the holes with good-quality, loamy soil.

SOIL TEXTURE

Soil texture affects how productive a soil may be and how easy it will be to manage. Some types of soil clump up when cultivated; other soil types are so porous that they don't hold water around plant roots.

The type and size of the particles in soil determine soil texture. Sandy soil is made up of large particles, so it has a coarse, gritty texture. It is easy to cultivate and allows nutrients and plant roots to pass through it readily. However, sandy soil dries out quickly.

Silt particles are smaller than sand and have a slippery texture, similar to talcum powder. Silty soil is less drought-prone because it retains water better than sandy soil. However, when silty soil dries out, it forms a hard surface, and water runs off instead of into the soil.

Clay is composed of microscopic particles. It tends to be sticky when wet, and nonporous. Because the particles form a crystalline structure, clay soil readily holds water and nutrients. Sometimes it holds too much water around plant roots. When dry, clay tends to clump together and form hard clods, which are difficult to cultivate and restrict the movement of plant roots through the soil profile. The soil surface becomes bricklike, preventing moisture and nutrients from entering.

Loam, the Cadillac of soils, contains a balanced mixture of all three particle types combined with organic matter, making the soil fertile, soft-textured, and rich. It has none of the drawbacks of the other soils.

PREPARING TO PLANT
continued

Most soils contain an excess of one particle type or another, which can cause problems for plant growth and cultivation.

CHECKING YOUR SOIL

To determine the particle makeup of soil in your yard, put a quarter cup of soil and a tablespoon of dishwasher soap in a pint jar and fill it with water. Shake the jar, then allow it to sit undisturbed until the soil has settled. Sand will fall to the bottom, silt will be next, followed by clay. Let the jar stand for 30 seconds, then measure the depth of the sand layer with a ruler. Wait 2 minutes, then measure the silt layer. After a couple of days, measure the clay layer. Divide the individual depths by the entire depth of soil in the jar. Multiply this number by 100 to determine the percentage of each particle type.

Loam will contain up to 52 percent sand, anywhere from 28 percent to 50 percent silt, and from 7 percent to 27 percent clay. If your soil is out of this general balance, amend it with organic matter.

An easier way to determine the soil's particle makeup is to dig at least a foot deep and examine the soil. You may find layers of different textures within the profile that would benefit from cultivating and mixing. Or you may find soft and crumbly soil, which means it should be fine for almost all plants. Or you may find that it is heavy and wet (clayey) or coarse and dry (sandy). Knowing this, you may want to choose plants that do well in clay or sand-based soils and adjust your irrigation and cultural practices to take this into account.

If you plan to amend your soil to improve soil texture, test it for soil nutrient content

Use the jar test method to determine the proportions of sand, silt, and clay in soil. The components separate into layers.

TESTING SOIL

The best way to determine a soil's nutrient needs is to test it. A test shows how much lime, sulfur, or fertilizer a bed requires.

You should test soil before planting, if possible, and you may want to test it periodically every few years after planting to ensure that nutrient balances remain in line with plant needs.

In most states, soil test kits and instructions are available from local extension offices and private laboratories. Testing fees are affordable and well worth the expense. Do-it-yourself soil test kits also are available and may be less expensive than laboratory tests. They're useful but not as specific and refined as laboratory tests.

TAKE THE TEST

These are general instructions for taking soil samples for a test. Contact the laboratory doing the test for any specific requirements and

information on how best to take and ship samples.

If possible, collect soil samples in late fall or early winter before the soil freezes. Then, if the soil requires lime or sulfur to alter pH, you can work it into the bed early enough that it has time to balance soil pH before planting. Also, because the spring planting rush is over at this time of year and labs are less busy, you should receive the results faster.

The way a sample is collected affects test accuracy. First, clean away any loose debris or mulch from the soil surface so these materials don't end up in the sample and skew results. Because every square foot of soil can be different, take a composite sample. Collect 15 to 20 uniform cores, or slices, of soil 6 inches deep from random spots in the bed. Get a good cross section of the area by taking cores in a zigzag pattern across the bed. Under trees and shrubs, take samples at the outer edge of branches or at drip lines.

Soil-coring tools are available, but a shovel, spoon or hand trowel works just fine for taking samples. Mix the samples together in a clean bucket. Only a pint of soil is used for the test, so take care to thoroughly mix the samples.

Soil testing is the only way to determine the nutrient needs of your soil and plants.

first. That way, any fertility needs can be addressed as you amend the soil.

IMPROVING SOIL QUALITY

Now that you know your soil's personality and needs, it is time to improve it so it can nourish your plants. In most cases, you'll add organic matter and fertilizer.

Organic matter is animal or plant material in various stages of decomposition. It improves soil structure by binding together soil particles. Clay soils become more porous with added organic matter, sandy soils less drought-prone. Organic matter also promotes the presence of microorganisms that break down later additions of organic materials and release nutrients. Soils rich in organic matter are dark brown to black in color.

You can use many organic materials for amending soil, including decayed leaves, sawdust, grasses such as straw and hay, peat moss, ground tree bark, lawn clippings, compost, and animal manure. Each provides similar advantages for your soil. Make your choice based on price and availability.

Sphagnum peat moss is for soils needing more moisture-holding capacity; it also lowers soil pH (makes it more acidic). Many cities and towns offer compost made from yard waste, such as leaves and lawn clippings, for free or a nominal fee. Others compost sewage waste. You can make compost at home, but probably in quantities too small for an entire landscape.

Agricultural waste, another source of organic matter for amending soil, can be inexpensive or free for the taking. It also may be richer in plant nutrients than other types of organic matter. Bedding material mixed with livestock or poultry manure makes a fine organic soil amendment, though never use fresh manure because it is high in salts and will burn young plants. Farms, processing companies, and cotton gins or mills also are other good sources of organic material.

Manures and other waste products may harbor weed seeds. Typically, if the materials have been properly composted, these seeds will have been killed. Ask the producer how they've handled the materials to learn whether you need to age or further compost it. A finished compost will be darker in color than fresh materials and will have a fresh, woodsy odor.

Sawdust and bark chips also can be used for organic matter; however, fresh sawdust competes with plants for nitrogen. Use only sawdust that has been composted for at least one year. Bark and sawdust don't have the water-holding capacity of other forms of organic matter; instead they improve soil aeration and general soil structure.

Amend ground cover beds with organic matter and fertilizer before planting.

HOW AND WHEN TO AMEND

Work organic matter into the soil. Ideally, you should amend the entire root zone to 12 inches deep, but realistically, tillers only dig 6 inches deep. If your soil is predominantly clay or sand, mix equal parts organic matter and soil (3 inches of compost tilled 6 inches deep). If your soil is loamy and already fertile and well-conditioned, add 1 part organic matter to 4 parts soil ($1\frac{1}{2}$ inches of compost). Spread the organic matter evenly over the soil surface, then incorporate it into the soil with a fork or tiller.

Ideally, you should add organic matter to a bed the fall before planting. Autumn is a dry season in most areas, so it's easier to till amendments into the soil then. Adding organic matter at this time gives several

PREPARING TO PLANT
continued

Install in-ground irrigation systems before you begin planting so that you won't have to disturb the plants.

them into the soil. But be aware that tilling reaches only 6 to 8 inches deep, and most root systems grow 12 inches deep.

If you are not working an entire bed, you can mix fertilizer directly into each planting hole. Blend it with the backfill soil.

UNDERSTANDING SOIL pH

Soil pH is measured on a scale of 0 to 14. A neutral soil has a pH of 7. Below 7, the pH is low and the soil is acidic; above 7, the pH is high and the soil alkaline.

pH affects soil fertility by governing the availability of nutrients in the soil. Some minerals, which are the basis of nutrients, are more soluble—and available—at low pH; others are more soluble under alkaline conditions. Most plants grow best in soil that has a pH of 6 to 7 because that's the range at which the greatest number of nutrients are available in optimum amounts. However, some ground covers, such as azaleas and mosses, prefer acid soils. Others, such as thyme and cinquefoil, prefer alkaline soils.

If soil pH is too acidic or alkaline, certain nutrients may not be available to plants, which results in poor growth and sometimes death. Also, certain plant diseases are more prevalent in acid or alkaline soil. For example, club root is more potent on rockcress when pH is low.

The only way to determine pH is through a soil test. Test results provide information on how much lime or sulfur your soil needs to raise or lower pH. Ground limestone raises the pH of acidic soils; sulfur reduces the pH of alkaline soils. Try to incorporate lime or sulfur into the soil several weeks to several months before planting. This allows time for these materials to be effective. Also, the more finely ground the material, the more soil particles it can contact and the faster the change will occur.

As you work the soil, remove any rocks and debris that rise to the soil surface.

months for it to affect soil structure. However, regardless of when you add organic matter, it's beneficial.

IMPROVING SOIL FERTILITY

Before amending the soil with materials to improve structure, test it to determine any specific nutrient needs. You'll want to know how much fertilizer your beds require before installing plants. And mixing fertilizer into the soil at the same time you amend saves time and energy.

Plants require certain nutrients to grow and thrive. They typically absorb most of these nutrients through their roots, though sometimes they absorb nutrients through their leaves and stems.

When applying fertilizer to a new bed, use an amount based on soil test recommendations. See page 28 for information on how to test soil. Spread the fertilizer over bare soil, followed by any amendments you're incorporating. Then work them into the soil's top 10 to 15 inches by digging or irrigating the area to dissolve the fertilizer. Or rototill

FINAL STEPS

If an irrigation system is in your plans, install it after working the soil. Afterwards, smooth the soil surface with a rake, removing any rocks and debris the rake brings up. With the rake, move excess soil from high points to fill low spots in the bed. Your goal is to create a flat surface, which will be more uniformly moist than one with dips. A wide aluminum landscape rake makes quick work of the job.

Your bed is ready to plant when it is weed-free, well-amended, and easy to work with your hands or hand tools.

FIRST THIS WORD

The key to low maintenance and successful gardening is choosing plants that are well-adapted to your climate and growing conditions. Often the best choices are plants that are indigenous to your area or nonnative plants that other local gardeners have tested and used successfully.

Native plants make sense because they essentially developed right in your own backyard, so they have evolved to survive under local weather patterns and typical disease and insect pressures. You don't have to pamper or protect native plants as much as you do imported or exotic plants because they are adapted to your environment. The only real disadvantage of using native plants is that some are so well-adapted to an area that they may be hard to control. See "Invasive Ground Covers," below, to help you identify potential problems. If you aren't sure which plants are native to your region, ask a local plant retailer or experienced gardeners for advice.

Pass-along plants, those given to you by fellow gardeners, are a fine source of plant material for ground covers. Pass-along plants are often free and can have sentimental value as well. Plus, you know you're getting plants that someone has already tested and found to work in your area.

However, exercise some caution when using pass-along plants. They may carry diseases or insect pests that can invade your landscape, or they may be generally unhealthy. Examine any pass-along plants, cuttings, or bulbs for signs of insects or disease, which may appear as discolored or damaged foliage or weak, underdeveloped root systems.

Before taking the plants, find out why they're being given away—they could be thugs—and if the person offering them has experienced any problems with them. Quarantine newly acquired pass-along plants for several weeks by planting them temporarily in pots or heeling them in away from other plants. See how they do in this environment. Transplant them permanently only after they pass this test.

INVASIVE GROUND COVERS

Some ground cover plants are so tough and fast-growing that they can overrun your yard. That's fine if you like the plant and don't mind it running wild. However, when ground covers invade other parts of the landscape, including the lawn, they are weeds and require work to control. Several ground cover species are notoriously rampant in practically any climate; others may be pests in certain regions where the conditions are especially conducive to their growth.

The thugs listed at right are fast-growing ground covers with a high potential for invasiveness. They are also some of the most common ground covers. Be aware that they may require supervision. You may need to install a physical barrier, such as a buried weed shield, to keep them in check, or you might need to mow or prune them more frequently than other ground covers. Most likely, though, you'll have to keep an eye on them and be ruthless at removing plants that overextend their bounds.

Some ground covers, such as these violets, can become invasive and may require extra maintenance to keep them in check.

PLANT THUGS

Ajuga
Baby's tears
Clematis
Creeping buttercup
   (*Ranunculus repens*)
Crown vetch (*Coronilla varia*)
English ivy
Goutweed
Honeysuckle
Knotweed (*Polygonum* spp.)
Lily-of-the-valley

Lippia
Mint
Mock strawberry
Moneywort
Sandwort
Sedum
Spotted dead nettle
Sweet woodruff
Wintercreeper
Vinca
Virginia creeper
Yellow archangel

BUYING PLANTS

Shop for ground covers at reputable suppliers. Choosing healthy plants initially ensures that your ground covers get a good start in life and will be long-lived in your landscape. Don't hesitate to ask for advice from the sales staff and your gardening friends.

After investing time, energy, and money in preparing your ground cover beds, you want to make doubly sure that you bring home plants that perform well. The following sections will help you select the healthiest plants and buy the right number of plants for your beds.

HOW MANY TO BUY

You can purchase plants before the ground cover bed is ready, but it's better to wait until you know the bed's final dimensions and can buy the correct number of plants to fill the space. That number depends on the spacing between plants. Generally, you leave as much space between plants as their mature size. Planting the ground covers somewhat closer together encourages faster coverage, while buying fewer plants and spacing them farther apart reduces pressure on your budget.

If plants are too far apart, weeds can emerge between them and compete for nutrients and water. It also takes longer to achieve complete coverage of the site. Planting them too closely can be a waste of time, money, and plant material. In addition, overcrowded plants compete with one another for nutrients and water.

Ultimately, plant vigor and size at maturity determine how rapidly ground covers fill an area. Your goal is to achieve full coverage of the bed by the third growing season.

Plants are spaced from center to center of each plant. A general spacing rule is one plant per square foot. Fast-growing species can be spaced farther apart than slow-growing plants, and larger plants, such as shrubs, should be spaced farther apart than more compact plants, such as grasses, strawberries, or thrift. For example, plants that grow slowly and do not have wide-spreading growth habits, such as pachysandra, English ivy, and vinca, can be as close as 6 inches apart. Quick-growing grasses should be about 8 inches apart. Ground cover shrubs, such as juniper or cotoneaster, may need as much as 3 feet of space—a mature-size spacing— to expand their branches.

Spacing recommendations in this book and elsewhere are based on achieving efficient coverage at a reasonable cost. But because plants don't grow uniformly across the country, ask local gardeners or nursery operators how the ground covers do in your locale and whether you should adjust the recommended spacing. Some ground covers may grow to larger or smaller sizes depending on your climate and other growing conditions, and you should take that into account in your planning.

The chart below shows how many plants it takes to fill a preset amount of space at standard spacing recommendations. If your ground cover bed is either a fraction or multiple of 100 square feet, you'll find it a simple matter to work with the number of plants in the 100-square-foot column. For example, a 25-square-foot bed requires 144 plants spaced 10 inches apart; a 500-square foot-bed takes 720 plants to fill.

To determine the exact number of plants for your bed, use this formula:

$$\text{Number of Plants} = \frac{\text{Area of Bed}}{\text{Recommended Spacing}^2}$$

ESTIMATING PLANT NUMBERS

Spacing (inches)	30 (sq. ft.)	100 (sq. ft.)	170 (sq. ft.)
4	270	900	1530
6	120	400	680
8	68	225	383
10	44	144	245
12	30	100	170
15	19	64	109
18	14	45	76
24	8	25	43

MEASURING YOUR GROUND COVER BED

Figuring the size and square footage of a square or rectangular bed is straightforward. Use standard geometric calculations. For other shapes, you'll have to use a bit more figuring. Here are the formulas to help.

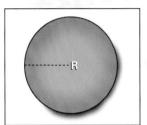

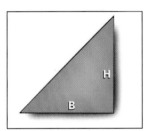

SQUARE OR RECTANGLE
Area = L times W
L = Length
W = Width

Example:
A = 90 feet × 60 feet
A = 5,400 square feet

CIRCLE
Area = $\pi \, r^2$
π = 3.14
r^2 = radius squared

Example:
A = 3.14 × 20 feet ×
    20 feet
A = 1,256 square feet

TRIANGLE
Area = 0.5 times B times H
B = Base
H = Height

Example:
A = 0.5 × 60 feet × 120 feet
A = 3,600 square feet

IRREGULAR SHAPES (accuracy within 5%)
Mark the length (L) of the area. Every 10 feet along the length line, measure the width (W) at right angles to the length line. Add up these measurements and multiply the result by 10.
    Example:
A = W1 + W2 + W3, etc. × 10
A = 35 + 71 + 26
A = 132 × 10
A = 1,320 square feet

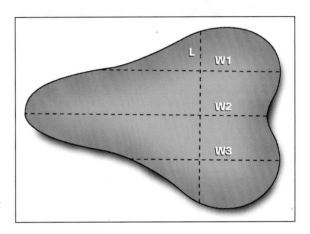

Measure the bed to be planted in inches. Calculate its area, keeping the units in inches (length × width = area). Then divide the area by the recommended spacing squared. (You'll find the standard spacings in the Plant Selection Guide.) Round up to the next whole number when the answer is a fraction. For example, the area of a bed that is 24 by 36 inches is 864 square inches. For a ground cover you plant 10 inches apart, divide the area by 100 (10 × 10). The answer is 8.64, so you need to buy nine plants.

WHERE TO BUY

Be discriminating about the plants you bring home. You can obtain free plants from friends and fellow gardeners, but follow the rules for pass-along plants to ensure you aren't bringing home problems. You can also purchase plants from local nurseries and garden centers or order them through the mail.
MAIL ORDER: Mail-order sources often have a wider selection of plant materials than

local nurseries, which typically carry only high-demand plant species due to limited storage and growing space. However, ordering plants by mail requires planning—you must time your order to ensure that plants arrive when you need them. You have less control over when mail-order plants will be available. They may arrive early, before your bed is ready to plant, or late, when they have less time to become established. And they may arrive in poor condition, depending on how they were packaged and handled during shipment. Mail-order ground covers also tend to be smaller than locally available plants because smaller plants are cheaper and easier to ship. If you use a mail-order source, check its reputation for quick, responsive service, high-quality products, and a plant guarantee. Ask experienced gardeners to recommend a reliable source of high-quality plant material.

The shipments should include proof that the nursery is certified as pest-free. As soon as mail-order plants arrive, unwrap them and check for signs of disease or damage. If plants

BUYING PLANTS
continued

Choose sturdy, healthy-looking plants, such as the one on the left, that are free of insects and diseases and not root-bound. The plant on the right, with its smaller size and less sturdy form, will take longer to establish.

arrive with problems, call the nursery to arrange a return. Some problems may crop up after you accept the shipment. These may result from poor handling practices or an infestation of insects or disease at the nursery, en route to your garden, or after arrival. If you receive plants that are damaged or diseased and you aren't sure of the cause, take them to your local extension office for evaluation.

Many mail-order plants are shipped bare-root—with no soil around their roots. They may be stressed from their travels and lack of water, so plant them as quickly as possible. If you can't plant them directly in the bed, plant them in pots or heel them into a holding bed and water them well. To heel in plants, dig a small trench that will accommodate the roots. Set plants in the trench, then snugly cover their roots with soil without compacting it. This provides a stable place for the ground covers to rest until you are ready to plant them permanently.

Plants are sold in many forms: bare-root, as seedlings in flats, and potted in containers of all sizes.

LOCAL NURSERIES: Purchase ground covers from a local dealer for better quality control and timing. When selecting plants, look for good color in their foliage and/or blooms. Plants should be lushly green with few or no yellow or brown leaves and stems. They also should exhibit vigorous growth. Look for dense, compact plants, which are hardier and likely to be healthier than long, leggy plants.

Before buying, check the plants for signs of insect infestation and disease, especially on the

undersides of leaves and at the nodes where leaves attach to stems. Look for insects at these places and for cuts or holes in the stems or leaves. Chlorotic (yellow) or brown areas can mean disease or insect damage. Examine the root system of at least one sample plant for insect and disease problems. While checking the roots, make sure the plant has plenty of them and that they are vigorous and not tightly matted or intertwined. Roots that are so tightly bound that you can't loosen them by gently massaging them between your fingers may never grow beyond the root ball.

PLANT PACKAGING

Typically, ground covers are sold in containers, either by the pot or by the flat. Spreading ground covers, such as pachysandra, ajuga, ivy, and many herbs, usually come in 2¼- to 4-inch containers. You can occasionally find them in flats of ground cover "sod"—the ground cover grows as a mass, and you cut it into pieces to fit your needs. Juniper, cotoneaster, and other large, woody ground cover shrubs are usually sold in 1- to 2-gallon pots. (A 1-gallon pot is similar in size to a 6-inch container.) Some nurseries may offer large ground covers as bare-root or balled-and-burlapped specimens.

Ground covers sold in flats or 2¼-inch pots tend to be small in size, but because they're less expensive than larger container plants, they're more affordable for large areas. They also tend to recover more rapidly from the stresses of moving and transplanting than larger plants. However, larger, more mature ground covers—those in 4-inch and bigger pots—quickly take root in their new home and spread to fill an area rapidly.

Bare-root plants have no growing medium around their root systems. They typically are available when dormant in winter and early spring. They are usually less vigorous than potted plants and may be slower to establish. They also may need more water initially to get their roots growing well. Balled-and-burlapped plants are sold with a large ball of earth around their roots bound in burlap cloth. Trees and shrubs are typically sold this way. They are easy to plant and should be just as healthy and vigorous as potted plants.

Plant bare-root ground covers as soon as you get them home. They often need extra care and watering for the first week or two after planting. Balled-and-burlapped plants can be left out of the soil for up to a week after purchase without much risk to the plant. However, be sure to water them if the weather is hot or dry. Container plants can be left in pots or flats for several weeks after purchase if you water them frequently.

PLANTING GROUND COVERS

Early spring is an ideal time to plant most herbaceous ground covers. The soil is easier to work then, especially in cold climates where the ground freezes in winter. Spring-planted ground covers are more likely to receive water from rain, which saves on your water bill as they become established. And early-spring planting allows the ground covers to become established before the next winter arrives.

Wait to plant in spring until any threat of a frost is past, the soil is fairly dry, and its temperature has reached at least 60° F. Soil is dry enough for planting if you can easily press a handful in your fist and it crumbles into smaller pieces when you release your grip.

Early fall is also another good time to plant, especially in areas where the soil is typically too wet to work in spring.

Dormant woody shrubs can be planted in winter if the soil isn't frozen. Avoid planting in summer unless you live in a mild climate. Heat and dry weather stress plants, making it difficult for them to become established. If you must plant ground covers in summer, take care to keep them adequately watered.

Whichever season you plant, the ground covers need plenty of time to become established before the onset of harsh, cold weather or extremely hot, dry weather.

LAYING OUT THE BED

You can lay out plants in standard rows—where plants are lined up behind one another—or in staggered (triangular) plantings (see the diagrams at right). Staggered planting provides faster, more even coverage and works better on slopes.

Use a ruler, tape measure, or spacing board (a board that is as long as the desired spacing) to mark the position of the holes, based on the spacing requirements of your plants. Spacing boards stay in place better than tapes. Leave the recommended spacing distance between the first row of plants and the edge of the bed.

To avoid obliterating the marks, start on one edge of the planting area and work your way across the bed to the other side. You can also work from the middle of the bed out. If you use this last technique, the middle of the bed is the center of the planting area. Mark the first row of plants at the bed's edge, then determine the center from that point. Adding extra plants at the corners of irregularly shaped beds helps ensure thorough coverage.

In a staggered pattern, the young plants line up like soldiers in diagonal rows, thus ensuring quick coverage.

If plants are in pots, set them on the position marks. You can leave them in place for several hours before planting, so you can jockey the plants around until all are perfectly spaced. But if planting bare-root ground covers or seedlings in cell packs, dig the holes and put the plant in the ground right away.

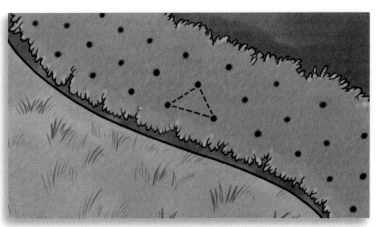

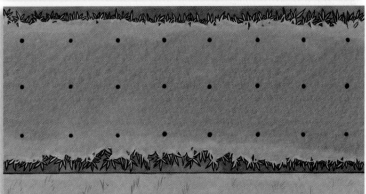

The two basic planting patterns—planting in rows (bottom) and staggered spacing (top)—make it easy to get fast, uniform coverage with your ground covers. Staggered spacing provides faster coverage and works better on slopes.

PLANTING GROUND COVERS
continued

Take care not to injure yourself when planting ground covers. Holding a trowel in this fashion will help protect your wrist from injury, especially when planting a large area, where the repetitive motions add up.

If you already have problems with your wrists, look for specialized trowels that will help prevent further damage.

Leaning over a bed can strain and injure your back. Always kneel. Plant the area within easy reach, then move to get the rest of the plants. Try to work your way around a bed so you're putting the least stress possible on your body.

EASY ON THE WRISTS

Digging just a few holes is not that taxing, but if you are planting a large area with many holes, your wrists can take a beating from the repetitive motion. A shovel, rather than a trowel, may be easier on them. Or if the holes are relatively small, use a trenching tool or other small-sized shovel.

If using a trowel, push it deeply in the soil and lift the dirt in an easy motion that does not stress your wrist. Go slowly and try to keep scoops small and light. Digging as though you were scooping with a spoon is particularly hard on wrists. Use the entire forearm in a fluid motion to avoid wrist injury when planting large numbers of ground covers. You may also want to wear a brace that keeps the wrist immobile.

Another technique is to grab the trowel handle with your thumb on top and the bowl of the trowel facing you (upper left). Dig by pulling the trowel toward you. This technique works best in well-prepared, friable soil.

If you already have problem wrists, try the trowel shown in the photo to the left. The grip forces you to keep your wrist straight; the optional brace helps immobilize the wrist even further. You'll find it takes a while to become comfortable using this trowel.

CONTAINER PLANTS

Holes should be deep enough that the plant's crown is right at or just above the soil level and wide enough to allow room to work as you set the plants in the hole. An inch on all sides should be enough for plants in small pots. For ground covers in 1- or 2-gallon containers, allow 2 inches on each side of the plant.

The hole for larger container plants should also be at a depth that keeps the top of the root ball at or slightly above the soil surface. If the container soil holds together, simply dig the hole and set the plant in place. But if the soil around these larger plants breaks up, form the soil in the middle of the bottom of the hole into a cone. Set the plant on this cone of soil and spread out its roots.

Handle plants with care when removing them from containers. Squeeze or press the bottom of the pot to push the plant out; do not pull by the stem. If a plant is snugly entrenched in its pot, turn the container over. With your hand supporting the plant at its base, lightly tap the edge of the pot against the edge of a table or other solid object to loosen the plant.

Carefully tease the outer roots of the root ball by hand or with a gentle spray of water. If the root ball is tightly matted, lightly massage it to loosen the roots before setting the plant in the hole. Spread the loosened roots in the hole. Refill the hole with soil and pack it firmly around the plant, but not so tightly that the soil becomes compacted.

BALLED-AND-BURLAPPED GROUND COVERS

Balled-and-burlapped plants can be planted much like large container plants. Leave natural burlap around the root ball—it will decompose in the soil—but loosen it slightly to give the roots a little elbow room. Some burlap is made from plastic, and some growers wrap the root ball with plastic before burlapping the ball. Completely remove these materials. Otherwise, roots may not grow out of the root ball. Also cut any twine that might be binding the burlap. It can girdle—strangle—roots and stems and kill the plant.

BARE-ROOT GROUND COVERS

Dig a hole deep enough that the uppermost roots sit at or just above the soil surface. The hole should be as wide as the roots' spread. As with large container plants, taper the soil in the hole to form a cone and spread the roots over the cone. Set the plant upright in the hole, then scoop backfill soil around its roots, tamping lightly to pack the soil around them. Pack soil firmly enough to support the plant, but don't compact it.

PLANTING ON SLOPES

You'll want to modify a steep slope so that water reaches plant roots and does not run off. To do this, create a basin around each plant, much as you do when planting a tree. Instead of building the basin all around each ground cover plant, though, simply mound soil higher on the downhill side to catch the water as it runs down the hill. You can also terrace the slope or install retaining walls made from lumber or cross ties. Terracing reduces runoff, protects against erosion, keeps water available to the plant, and makes it easier for you to navigate the slope.

AFTER CARE

When all plants are in place, water the area gently and thoroughly so that it settles the soil and seeps into the root zone. Then mulch the bed to secure the soil and retain moisture.

Mulching is especially important on slopes because it helps prevent soil from eroding as plants establish. On steep slopes, landscape fabric can help hold soil in place. Install it before planting, then dig holes through the fabric as you plant. Roll the fabric down the hill and secure it with metal stakes or pins.

Ground covers need plenty of moisture to get them off to a good start and alleviate transplanting stress. Water plants at least weekly for the first three to four weeks after planting, or whenever they show any sign of wilting. Once they are established, most ground covers can be irrigated less frequently.

Terracing a slope controls soil erosion, ensuring that ground covers receive adequate water. Cut into the slope to create a level surface; use the soil you remove to build up the slope below the cut and form a terrace. Until the ground covers establish, hold soil in place with landscape fabric.

WEEDING AND MULCHING

Mulching ground cover beds after installation helps plants thrive. After establishment, mulching benefits the plants by holding water near their roots.

When ground covers are established, they require just some basic maintenance, including weeding, mulching, fertilizing, watering, pruning or mowing, and sometimes thinning.

WEEDING

Although individual plants may establish quickly, it takes time for the beds to fill in. For that reason, weeding is vital in the early years of a ground cover bed's life. Although you worked hard to eliminate weeds before planting, they will still pop up. Even well-established beds can become weedy. Vines, with their loose growth habits, are especially prone to letting weeds encroach.

If left unchecked, weeds can take over both new and well-filled-in beds. Check beds weekly, especially in the growing season, to catch weeds as they emerge. Then it's simple to hoe or pull them.

Weeds are easiest to pull, and displace the least soil as you pull them, when the soil is moist. So weed after watering or after a rain. Remove the entire plant, roots and all, by grasping it close to its base and pulling in an even motion. This helps prevent the weed's top from snapping off, leaving its roots to regrow. Wear gloves with rubber grips; they provide a better hold on the weed as well as protect your hands.

To remove deeply rooted weeds, use a fish-tail weeder (also called an asparagus knife or dandelion fork). Slip the tool under the weed's roots, then pry the entire plant out of the ground. Remove pulled weeds from the bed so they can't reroot.

You can also control the weeds with herbicides, especially postemergence products. The trick to using herbicides effectively and safely in established beds is to select the right herbicide for your needs. Look for products that are specific to the weed problem and are safe to use on the ground cover. For example, a grass-specific herbicide, such as fluazifop, can be sprayed over broad-leaved ground covers to control bermudagrass without harming the ground cover. An herbicide's label should clearly state which weeds it will control and which plants it can be used on.

Follow label directions explicitly and apply herbicides on still days so wind won't blow them onto ornamental plants. In some cases, you may be able to cover neighboring plants before applying herbicides to the weeds to limit exposure to drift. If you need help selecting the right herbicide or understanding application rates and rules, contact your local extension agent.

MULCHING YOUNG PLANTINGS

Mulching is invaluable for new plantings. It suppresses weeds by preventing light from reaching the soil surface. Weeds that do break through the mulch are easy to spot and usually easy to pull. A layer of mulch maintains moisture in the soil near the ground covers' roots and keeps soil cool in summer. Organic mulches enrich soil with humus and nutrients as they decompose.

Apply mulch in spring after the soil has warmed, spreading it thickly and evenly. To aid plant growth, spread fertilizer over the bed before mulching or mix the recommended amount into the mulch.

In cold climates, cover new plantings, especially fall-planted ones, with a winter mulch to protect them from freezing. Spread the mulch before the first hard freeze. This keeps the ground warm and gives fall-planted ground covers more time to establish before winter arrives.

The greatest risk to established plants in winter is not the freezing but the soil thawing and refreezing. For established ground covers, apply the mulch after the ground has frozen. Mulched soil is more likely to stay frozen and keep plants dormant even during warm spells.

Winter mulch materials include pine needles and evergreen boughs. Apply a loose,

4- to 6-inch-deep layer over the plants. This insulates the plants and protects them from cold, dry winter wind. Don't apply mulch so thick that it mats and smothers plants.

MULCHES

Here are a few of the many organic materials available for mulching.

■ **WOOD PRODUCTS:** Chipped or shredded bark—usually fir, pine, or redwood—makes an excellent, attractive mulch. Its texture ranges from fine to coarse. Bark chips and shredded bark are readily available in small bags or in bulk. They may be more expensive than other mulches, but they are long-lasting.

The size of the chips to use depends on availability and personal taste. Large chips allow more air and water movement through the soil because they don't mat against the soil surface. They also let in more light, so weed seeds can germinate. Smaller chips may work better around low-growing ground covers or ones with finely textured foliage because they readily filter through the leaves.

Sawdust is an inexpensive mulch; in some areas, you can even get it for free. But it is not as attractive as bark products, and it tends to tie up the nitrogen in the soil as microbes break it down. If you use sawdust, buy a product that is fortified with nitrogen, or add additional nitrogen to your beds at a rate of ½ pound per 100 square feet of raw sawdust mulch. Apply sawdust mulch 1 inch deep.

■ **PINE NEEDLES:** Pine needles—also called pine straw—are readily available and very attractive. They can be expensive if bought in bales; free pine straw may be available from your own yard or from neighbors. Pine-needle mulches last for several years and are ideal for ground covers that prefer acid soil, such as azaleas.

■ **STRAW, HAY, AND GRASS CLIPPINGS:** These readily available mulches are effective and free, but they are less attractive than pine bark and needles. They degrade rapidly, so you must replenish them frequently. Their coarse texture makes them troublesome to apply at even depths because they mound up easily, and they often contain weed seeds.

■ **TREE LEAVES:** Leaves are free and readily available. Collect them from your yard as you rake in autumn. They tend to degrade rapidly and blow about more than other mulches, so heavy, thick leaves work best. Shredded leaves stay in place better and are more aesthetic as well.

Heavy, coarse-textured leaves, such as those of oaks, typically provide a looser mulch than light leaves, such as maples, which tend to mat down. For that reason, heavy, coarse-textured leaves make a good winter mulch.

Oak leaves are acidic and are an excellent mulch for acid-loving plants. To use lighter-weight leaves, shred or chop them so they will be less likely to blow around.

■ **COMPOSTED MANURE:** Manure is a rich source of nutrients and is often easy to obtain. You can sometimes get it free from local stables and farms. Processed or composted, bagged manure is available from retail outlets.

Fresh manure is high in salts and nutrients that can burn plants. It may also contain grass and weed seeds, which will germinate in your beds. Make sure stable manure is properly composted, not just aged. Proper composting, in which the pile heats up to at least 160° F, kills weed seeds. Packaged, processed manure is usually seed-free. Even though processed, it can be high in salts. Manure mulches must be replenished about once a year.

■ **NEWSPAPER PRODUCTS:** Old newspapers are effective, cheap, and readily available. They are excellent for suppressing weeds and retaining moisture in the soil, but they are unattractive and, when wet, can mat around plants. They last only one season. Save papers at your house and lay them in sheets around plants, or shred them for a fluffier mulch.

A new product, which currently has limited regional distribution, is newspaper processed into nuggets. It is more attractive than homemade newspaper mulches.

You can also improve aesthetics by laying sheets of newspaper around plants and covering them with another mulch, such as bark chips. Not only will it look better, you will be adding organic matter to the area.

■ **ORGANIC BYPRODUCTS:** Corncobs, mushroom compost, peanut or pecan hulls, cotton gin trash, waste sludge, and many other byproducts of agriculture and industry are excellent mulches and may be available for free or a small fee in your area. These mulches vary in nutrient and organic matter content but are quite attractive and effective, as well as long-lived in the landscape. Check for local sources of these products.

Cocoa hulls, which are also available commercially, have a delicious scent when fresh, and they are an excellent source of potassium. However, they can be expensive, and they mold in wet situations. There are reports of them being toxic to dogs.

Landscape fabric is one of the best physical weed controls in ground cover beds. Roll the fabric over the bed; hold it in place with landscape pins. Cut slits to plant through. After planting, hide the fabric under a layer of mulch.

FERTILIZING

Spring is the best time to fertilize ground covers. You can easily fertilize small beds by hand. Wearing a mask is not a necessity, but it keeps the dust out of your nose.

Typically, woody ground covers require less fertilizer than herbaceous ground covers, but all benefit from an occasional dose. The three primary nutrients that ground covers and all plants need are nitrogen, phosphorus, and potassium (N, P, K for short). Nitrogen affects a plant's growth and its ability to form leaves, buds, and flowers. Phosphorus provides energy and promotes root development, growth, and fruiting. Potassium increases plant vigor and strength, encourages early root development, and increases resistance to disease and environmental stress.

High-nitrogen fertilizers—those with a 2:1:1 or 3:1:1 ratio (see page 42)—promote vegetative growth and less flowering and fruiting. Applying them to new ground cover

beds helps plants grow fast and quickly fill in the bed. At this stage, coverage is more important than flowering, even with a ground cover you planted for its blossoms. When the bed is established, switch to a more balanced product—one with a 1:1:1 ratio—or one with higher phosphorus, such as a 1:2:1 ratio— to ensure flowers and fruit.

Plants also require micronutrients, such as magnesium and iron. These are called micronutrients because plants require them only in tiny amounts; however, they are as vital as primary nutrients. Soil usually contains all the micronutrients a plant needs; commercial synthetic and organic fertilizers usually provide them, too, as does organic matter. But some regions are prone to micronutrient deficiencies; a soil test will indicate if this is so for your garden.

In particular, iron deficiency is common. Iron is used in the production of chlorophyll and for several enzyme functions. Alkaline soil and soggy, poorly drained soil inhibit iron uptake. In alkaline soil, iron forms an insoluble compound with calcium that is unavailable to plants. Researchers are learning that iron can be nearly as important as primary nutrients and that applications often help green up plants, even when nitrogen is not deficient.

CLUES YOU NEED TO FERTILIZE

If the growth of established ground covers is sluggish and they show the following symptoms, they probably need fertilizer.
NITROGEN: Nitrogen-deficient ground covers have pale greenish-yellow leaves and stunted growth. Signs of nitrogen deficiency usually appear first in older leaves, which are the lowest leaves on the plant or its stems.
PHOSPHORUS: A phosphorus-deficient ground cover will be slow-growing and stunted, and its leaves may be dark green or purplish in color.
POTASSIUM: Potassium-deficient ground covers are spindly and poorly developed; taller-growing ground covers may fall over. Deficient plants are susceptible to leaf and stem diseases. Though rare, severe potassium deficiencies cause leaves to curl and brown around the edges starting at the tip. Symptoms usually begin with the leaves lowest on the plant stem and move up.
IRON: Iron-deficient plants become chlorotic, with all of the leaf except its veins turning yellow. Symptoms start at leaf edges and usually affect new leaves first.

FERTILIZERS

Fertilizers are available in a wide, and often confusing, array of choices. They come in many forms—organic and synthetic, fast-release and slow-release, dry and liquid. Each type has advantages and disadvantages, and some types are more appropriate in certain situations than in others.

Because ground covers hug the soil, fertilizing them is trickier than other, more upright and freestanding plants. You'll need to apply fertilizer over the top of ground cover plants rather than directly to the soil at their bases. For that reason, choose a fertilizer that will not burn the foliage.

The best fertilizers for ground covers come in small granules or liquid form. These products will work their way through or be directly absorbed by the foliage, so plenty of nutrients reach the plants. Whether you choose an organic or a synthetic fertilizer is a matter of personal taste. Understand the pros and cons of each before you decide.

Organic fertilizers rarely burn plants. They are slower-acting because they release nutrients only after microbes break down the fertilizer into individual chemicals—a process dependent on the weather (it takes warm temperatures and moisture). So organic fertilizers release nutrients gradually over time rather than all at once. Although they take longer to affect plant growth, they are available to plants longer than some synthetic fertilizers. In other words, if your plants have a nutrient deficiency, organic fertilizers won't be a quick fix. But they provide a small amount of nutrients at a slow, steady pace and contribute to a rich microflora in the soil.

The nutrient content of organic fertilizers is generally low, and it can be difficult to know their precise nutrient content, especially with homemade fertilizer such as manure tea (made from soaking manure in water). Some organic fertilizers may contain high concentrations of one nutrient and be deficient in others. However, processed organic fertilizers, such as Milorganite (sewage sludge), are available in uniform pellets and have been tested and labeled with their nutrient content, so you'll have a more precise picture of what your plants are getting.

Synthetic fertilizers are manufactured products and are generally made from inorganic substances. They come in a variety of forms, from dry powders or granules to water-soluble emulsions and liquids. Many of the dry, granulated fertilizers are inexpensive and release their nutrients as soon as they dissolve, providing immediate benefits to the plants but also dissipating rapidly. Synthetic fertilizers often are easier to apply than organic ones because they are not as bulky, and they provide exact levels of nutrients to your plants. They tend to be more potent than organic fertilizers.

Fertilize mature or established ground covers with a product containing nitrogen, phosphorus, and potassium in a ratio of 1:1:1 or 1:2:1. This 16-25-12 fertilizer is close; it has a 1.3:2:1 ratio.

Quick-release forms, such as ammonium nitrate, contain salts, which can burn roots and leaves. They are also highly soluble, so they readily move beyond the root zone, especially in rainy weather. After applying them to ground covers, take care to water thoroughly to wash them off foliage. You can expect effects to last from two to six weeks.

Slow-release synthetic formulations, such as methylene urea, ureaformaldehyde, or coated products such as sulfur-coated urea or Poly-S (polymer-coated), gradually release nutrients throughout the growing season and are less likely to burn plants or have their nutrients move out of the root zone. They can supply nutrients for three to nine months, depending on the product. Many of the fertilizers on the market are a combination of slow and fast-release materials. They quickly correct nutrient deficiencies and provide a long-term supply of nutrients.

LIQUID FORMULATIONS

Liquid fertilizers are readily absorbed by plant leaves, stems, and roots and are convenient to apply. (Dry fertilizers must dissolve in the soil before they're available to roots.) Although liquid fertilizers are more expensive than dry formulations, especially for fertilizing large areas, they can provide a quick, short-term

FERTILIZING
continued

Fertilizer spreaders provide a uniform, easy method of applying granular fertilizer, especially for large areas.

remedy for nutrient deficiencies.

With so many choices, first determine your plants' needs, then use a formulation that fits them. If your plants need a quick pick-me-up, fast-release fertilizers and liquid fertilizers that are absorbed directly into the leaves and stems may be best. If you want nutrients to reach your plants slowly and over time, slow-release synthetic or organic fertilizers are a better choice.

FERTILIZER FACTS

The three hyphenated numbers on fertilizer labels are a clue to how much of the three major nutrients are in the package. A package of 10-10-10 contains 10 percent nitrogen, 10 percent phosphorus, and 10 percent potassium. Such a fertilizer is called "balanced" because the nutrients are mixed in a ratio of 1:1:1. A 5-10-5 fertilizer has a ratio of 1:2:1 and is 5 percent nitrogen, 10 percent

phosphorus, and 5 percent potassium.

Ground covers grown for their foliage need a fertilizer with more nitrogen and potassium than phosphorus, so choose a product with a ratio of 2:1:2, such as a 10-5-10 fertilizer. Ground covers that are grown for their flowers do better with a balanced fertilizer or one with a 1:2:1 ratio.

Fertilizer labels don't always state specific application rates for ground covers. A rate of 1½ pounds of nitrogen per 1,000 square feet is a good general rule. However, it's best to ask a plant professional, an extension agent, or nursery staff for guidelines for your ground cover plants and situation.

Don't overapply fertilizers! That can injure plants by burning leaves and roots. Salts in quick-release materials pull water out of the plants. Unprocessed organic fertilizers rarely offer specific application rates or nutrient ratios, but they are less likely to damage plants if overapplied. However, applying too much fertilizer—whether it's organic or synthetic—wastes time and money, so use only what is required.

HOW TO FERTILIZE

Apply an annual booster dose of fertilizer just before plants start their growing season (early spring in most areas). Fertilize when leaves are dry so the fertilizer doesn't adhere to them.

In newly planted beds where bare ground is visible, you can sidedress plants with the fertilizer. Sprinkle it around the plants, then scratch it in with a cultivator, or water it in.

On established plantings, broadcast the fertilizer over the top of the plants. Using a push spreader ensures even coverage, but because it is difficult to push a spreader over some ground covers, a hand rotary spreader works almost as well. You can also broadcast the fertilizer by hand, but this is the least accurate method.

Immediately and thoroughly, water in the fertilizer so it won't burn plants. If you're using a slow-release or organic product, you can ignore this step. However, even though neither slow-release nor organic materials burn foliage, they are combined with quick-release materials in some fertilizer products. Unless you're sure of what you have, go ahead and water.

Ground covers with leaves that grow in whorls around the stem, such as ajuga, or that form thick clumps, such as ornamental grasses, may trap fertilizer granules in their foliage. Take extra care to wash quick-release fertilizer granules off these plants. For these plants, it's easier to use liquid fertilizers or slow-release products.

In large areas that are inaccessible to a push spreader, you can broadcast fertilizer by hand. The trick to uniform coverage is to overlap passes by about a third. Try practicing the technique on a driveway using sand as the broadcast material.

GROOMING BEDS

Although most ground covers need little grooming, occasionally you must give them some attention to spruce up their appearance by eliminating dead foliage and, in some cases, to keep the plants under control.

One of the easiest ways to perk up a ground cover bed is to mow it. You can do this after winter before plants break dormancy. Mowing rejuvenates growth and removes dead or spent leaves and stems. It also prevents organic "trash" from building up between the foliage and the soil.

Mowing is not an option for tall ground covers and ones with tough, woody growth, but it works well for low-growing herbaceous ground covers, such as ajuga, ivy, and lilyturf. It's a fast way to clean up spent, winter-tired foliage, especially in large beds. Grooming tall or vining and woody ground covers generally requires hand-pruning. Pruning removes less plant material than mowing and lets you control the shape of the plant.

Rake leaves from ground cover beds in fall, if the leaves tend to mat down. In cold areas, wait till spring to rake; the leaves serve as winter mulch.

WHEN TO GROOM

Generally, mow and prune each year just before the growing season begins or soon after plants bloom. Most ground covers need only a little trimming to maintain a uniform, compact shape. Some, such as cotoneasters, need grooming only every few years when (or if) they become straggly or produce many upright shoots.

Vines grow rapidly and may take over an area if not trimmed back several times each year. Honeysuckle especially requires constant attention to prevent it from becoming a tangle of growth or strangling trees and other plants around it.

Check the care instructions section for each plant in the Plant Selection Guide to determine the specific times to prune or mow ground covers. If you mow them, set the mower to its highest mowing height so you don't scalp the plants or cut into the soil. Use a bagger to collect debris.

SLOPES

Trimming slopes can be especially tough. They often are too steep to mow safely—which is why you planted ground cover instead of lawn—and if they are terraced, their terrain is too uneven for a mower to maneuver or make smooth cuts. Although these areas can be hand-sheared or pruned, using a string trimmer on them is much easier. Keep the trimmer at a uniform height above the ground to make even cuts. Some ground cover plants, especially woody shrubs, may have stems that are too tough to cut with a string trimmer; these you may have to prune by hand. Or trim them often enough that you always cut young, tender growth.

Mowing makes quick work of cleaning up a large bed of low-growing herbaceous ground covers. Usually, the mower blade height should be raised so you won't scalp the plants.

WATERING

All ground covers, even drought-tolerant ones, need an occasional sprinkling. How much they need depends on plant type, root depth, climate, and soil conditions. The Plant Selection Guide gives general water recommendations for each plant. Fine-tune them according to your site.

When first planted, ground cover beds require light, frequent irrigation because they depend on the water supply in the immediate vicinity of their small root systems. At this stage of growth, the soil should be kept constantly moist so that the plants don't wilt.

Once the plants are established and their root systems cover more area, you can water less. Unless you live in an arid region or the plants require high levels of moisture, irrigate only when the plants begin to wilt or show signs of stress.

Impulse sprinklers throw water in a circular pattern. Most models can be adjusted to water in partial circles.

HOW MUCH WATER?

Water established plants deeply and infrequently. Apply an inch or more of water at a time, every week or two. This promotes deep root growth, which makes the plants better able to survive drought. Typically, 1 inch of rain will soak 12 inches into sandy soil, 7 inches into loam, and 4 to 5 inches into clay soil.

Determine the watering rate of your sprinkler or irrigation system so you know how long to let the water run to put down an inch (see page 45). Sprinklers deliver between ½ inch and 2 inches of water per hour, depending on the size of the nozzles. The rate at which soaker hoses and drip sprinklers apply water depends on the number of holes in the tubing or the size of the emitter, as well as the water pressure.

Soak the bed every week or two during warm weather. Your goal is to keep the root zone of the plants—usually the top 8 inches of soil—moist but not wet. The soil surface may dry but not the root zone. How long the soil remains moist depends on its texture and the weather. Clay soil retains water longer than other soils, so you won't have to irrigate as often. Sandy soil doesn't hold water and requires more irrigation.

In cool, moist climates, you won't need to water as often as you would in hot, dry regions. Extremely arid or hot regions require frequent watering. In cold climates, water regularly until the ground freezes; plants that are not drought-stressed better withstand freezing.

Too much water is as harmful as too little. If plants growing in moist soil wilt in bright sunlight, drop leaves prematurely, or show signs of rot, you are watering too much.

WATERING SLOPES

Irrigating ground cover beds on slopes can be tricky. Soil on slopes erodes easily, especially when beds are young and haven't filled in. Because water is more likely to run down the slope than soak in even in established beds, standard irrigation methods result in slopes that are dry on the top and wet at the base.

Set up sprinklers to water in stages. Irrigate until the water begins to run off the surface. Check the edges of the slope to monitor runoff. When runoff begins, cut off the water supply for about 20 minutes to let the water soak into the soil. Repeat this process until the soil is thoroughly soaked.

In many situations, an automatic system is best. Drip sprinklers can apply water slowly and directly onto the soil. If you install a pop-up system, select different-sized nozzles so that more water is applied at the top of the slope, less in the center, and little at the base.

WHEN TO WATER

To check soil moisture, wait 24 hours after a thorough soaking and dig down 6 to 12 inches into the root zone. You can see how moist the soil is by looking at it—it should be dark colored—or by extracting a clump of soil and squeezing it in your palm. If the soil won't form a ball and crumbles easily, it is too dry. If it forms a ball but doesn't crumble, it's wet. Adjust watering accordingly. You can also monitor water with a moisture meter purchased from a nursery or hardware store and embedded in the soil.

Water early in the morning if possible so that foliage dries before nightfall. Watering at night leaves moisture on plant foliage and stems for extended periods of time, which, especially in humid regions, promotes disease and pest problems.

Oscillating sprinklers water in a rectangular pattern. Because they shoot water high into the air, wind easily deflects the pattern.

IRRIGATION SYSTEMS VS. SPRINKLERS

To irrigate ground covers, you can use a standard hose-end sprinkler, either hand-held or with a portable, freestanding, pivoting or rotating sprinkler. But an automatic irrigation system provides a more accurate, uniform water supply and frees you from spending hours holding a hose or moving the hose and sprinklers around.

Sprinklers and hoses are much less expensive to buy than in-ground irrigation systems, but they don't apply water as efficiently or as uniformly. As much as a fourth of the water they put out evaporates before reaching the soil. And they tend to apply more water near the sprinkler head, less on the outer edges of its spray.

To determine a sprinkler's distribution pattern and the time it takes to apply a set amount of water, place flat-bottomed containers that are the same size (buckets or cans work well) on the ground within the sprinkler's watering range. To test for uniformity of coverage, run the sprinkler for 15 minutes, then measure the water in each container. If the difference in water levels is more than ¼ inch among the containers, move the sprinkler frequently to ensure full coverage. For application rates, time how long it takes the sprinkler to fill the containers with an inch of water, then time irrigations based on that measurement.

SOAKER HOSES AND DRIP SYSTEMS

If you live where water is scarce, drip irrigation and soaker hoses are good because they put water directly on the root systems, so little water is lost to evaporation. Both emit water along the lengths of their tubing. They don't splash water droplets or wet foliage, so they reduce the chance of disease spreading from plant to plant. They also reduce the potential for soil erosion because water soaks slowly and directly into the soil rather than flowing over the surface, which can lead to runoff. For that reason, drip systems and soaker hoses are ideal to use on slopes.

Both soaker hoses and drip systems apply water very slowly. They can take several hours longer to apply the same amount of water as a sprinkler. So be sure to let them run long enough to adequately water plants.

Soaker hoses can be moved around to different areas, much like a portable sprinkler. Drip irrigation systems are usually more permanent, remaining in place for several years. They can be laid on the soil surface or buried under a few inches of soil or mulch. You also can install more complicated systems consisting of emitters, PVC pipe, and hoses or porous tubing. Hook them to timers and equip them with fertilizer injectors to further increase efficiency and save labor.

In ground cover beds, drip systems work best among plants with central growing points as opposed to dense plantings. In dense plantings, it is difficult to fix clogged emitters or replace broken parts without harming plants. For these situations, consider a pop-up irrigation system.

Place drip and soaker hoses 12 to 18 inches apart for small plants, no more than 12 inches apart on slopes or droughty soils. In cold climates, aboveground hoses should be drained and stored indoors to prevent freezing.

Although drip systems are more expensive than soaker hoses and sprinklers, they often pay for themselves in the long run by reducing labor and water usage.

POP-UP SYSTEMS

Pop-up or raised-head irrigation systems consist of PVC pipes with sprinkler heads that rise just above the foliage. They are ideal for closely spaced plants or plants that form a dense mat across the soil, such as ivy and vinca. The best nozzle heads for ground covers are those that produce a gentle mist.

A well-designed system should evenly apply water to the bed with little waste. Take care to irrigate on calm days to ensure uniform coverage.

PESTS AND PEST CONTROL

In plantings of broad-leaved ground covers, grassy weeds can often be controlled with herbicides that are specific to grasses, such as fluazifop.

Ground covers in general are low-maintenance plants with few insect or disease problems. As with all plants, though, there are exceptions to the rule. Some ground covers are highly susceptible to certain pests. For example, crown gall disease and scale insects frequently attack wintercreeper.

The pests that attack ground cover species are as diverse as the plants themselves. Among them are insects such as aphids, mites, caterpillars, and scales, and powdery mildew, wilts, blights, rusts, molds, and anthracnose diseases. Pests that thrive in thick, moist plant growth, such as slugs, can be especially serious.

CONTROLLING PESTS

Rarely is it possible to eliminate all pests in a landscape; instead, managing them is the key to success. One way to do that is with integrated pest management (IPM). With this approach, you coordinate cultural, physical, biological, and chemical methods of control.

Determining when to act decisively against a pest by spraying pesticides and when to apply cultural or biological controls takes time and education. Learn which pests can be problems for your ground covers, the point at which natural controls no longer work, and what methods are available for managing the pests. Be aware that when using an IPM approach, you must be willing to accept the presence of some pests in your landscape.

Using IPM puts you in control. Instead of reaching for a pesticide the moment you see a problem, you first examine the circumstances, then select the most appropriate control. You realize that a few beetles chewing holes in the leaves of two or three plants may be nothing to get excited about. But if the insects are on a fourth of the bed or more, or if a fast-moving pest such as spider mites has taken hold, you know it is time to take action.

STEPS OF IPM

The first step in IPM is to plant insect- and disease-resistant ground covers, especially if your area is prone to certain pests or diseases.

Then take time to learn about any potential problems. An extension agent can tell you what to expect and the levels of damage the plants can tolerate. He or she can point out the kind of damage a pest causes and how serious a problem it can be. The tolerance to pests varies among plant species, so ask a professional about limits and parameters. Besides knowing what the plant can take, you also need to decide how much damage to the plant *you* can tolerate.

Step three involves consistent monitoring. Watch for problems and identify the cause of any that arise (disease, insect, animal, or cultural). Estimate the scope of the problem and look for the presence of natural predators that may help control pests for you.

Step four is to choose a control. If damage reaches the point of action, a combination of control measures, from a change in cultural practices to applying pesticides to using alternative methods, helps avoid pesticide resistance and reduce predator populations. When pest populations are low, a cultural control such as increasing watering frequency may be all that is necessary. If cultural controls do not work or if the problem is out of hand, turn to pesticides, either biological or chemical, depending on the problem.

The fifth and final step is to analyze the effectiveness of your chosen control. If your control measures seem to be working, you can relax a bit. But if not, try another approach. Again, seek advice from professionals whenever you are in doubt.

YOUR IPM ARSENAL

CULTURAL CONTROLS: One of the best defenses against pests is healthy plants, which is more of a prevention than a cure. Proper cultural practices, such as fertilizing and irrigating plants in a timely manner, can keep pests from doing major damage to plants.
PHYSICAL CONTROLS: Pruning to improve air circulation cuts down on many diseases and some insect pests. Dividing

overcrowded plants also helps keep pests and diseases from developing.

Hand-pick larger pests such as scale insects, slugs, snails, and caterpillars. Mulch to prevent water splashing on leaves, which can help reduce some diseases. Set out traps to snare insects, such as moths, worms, and beetles. The traps are baited with natural chemical messengers, which are based on insect pheromones. Be aware, however, that they can attract pests to an area. Rather than being a control, they let you know when it's time to take action against arriving pests.

Sometimes you also have to be ruthless and remove affected plants. It's always better to toss a few diseased plants than let the disease spread through the bed. Replace them with ground covers that are resistant to the pest.

PREDATORS: Many predator insects exist naturally in gardens. Companies offer them for sale for you to release in your landscape. Among the best predators are parasitic wasps, ladybugs (or lady beetles), lacewings, predator mites, and parasitic nematodes.

Aphytis melinus and *Metaphycus helvolus* are tiny parasitic wasps that control scale insects. They lay eggs on the scale; the larvae hatch and feed on the scale, killing it. Trichogramma wasps do the same to caterpillars. Ladybugs attack and kill a wide range of insect pests, including spider mites, small worms, aphids, and other soft-bodied insects. Lacewings feed on many of the same insect pests. Predatory mites kill the spider mites that attack plants. Parasitic nematodes such as *Steinernema* control ground-living insect pests, including cutworms, grubs, and weevils.

If you decide to use predators, remember that they are living organisms. You can't simply store them in the garage and pull them out when you have problems. For them to be effective, you must provide the right environmental conditions, both in storage and in the landscape when you apply them. Your supplier should be able to advise you.

BIOLOGICAL PESTICIDES: Organic insecticides such as Bt and neem act against specific pests. For example, one form of the bacteria Bt, or *Bacillus thuringiensis*, kills caterpillars by attacking the lining of their stomachs. Organic insecticides usually leave the beneficial insect population intact.

Insecticidal soap reduces populations of soft-bodied insects, such as aphids and mites. Pyrethrin, rotenone, and neem are pesticides that come from plants. Like all pesticides, they can be toxic to humans and other vertebrates and to beneficial insects.

Homemade pesticides, such as garlic sprays, act more as repellents and, as such, can keep some pests out of your ground cover beds. Dormant and horticultural oil sprays smother pests such as scale and mites.

INORGANIC PESTICIDES: Chemical controls are faster-acting and more effective than biological and physical controls. Select materials labeled for your specific pest or disease and follow all label directions.

Pesticides act in three ways: systemically— they are absorbed by the plant and kill pests that feed on plant tissue and sap; by contact— they kill the pests they contact; and by leaving a residue on the plant's surface—they kill insects as they eat foliage and blooms.

Many products, both synthetic and biological, are available for controlling pests. Match the product to the pest and the situation. Handle all pesticides with care.

PESTS AND PEST CONTROL
continued

Euonymus scale attacks wintercreeper plantings by the thousands. It is only one of many insects that can affect ground cover beds. Most are specific to the plant, but some, such as snails, slugs, spider mites, and nematodes, are general feeders.

Moles and other rodents become problems in ground covers, in part because ground cover beds provide a hospitable environment. Often the best defenses against wildlife are repellents, physical barriers, or traps.

Powdery mildew is a disease that affects many plants, especially in humid conditions. Treat it as rapidly as possible. Improving air circulation by thinning surrounding plants will help.

Pesticides can kill friendly organisms that might help you battle the pests. Before spraying, check the predator population in your landscape.

POTENTIAL PESTS

Nematodes are microscopic, soilborne roundworms that attack roots, weakening and sometimes killing the plant. They are most severe in the Southeast. If ground covers have plenty of water and nutrients but aren't thriving, check their roots for signs of withering or for galls (hard, swollen lumps on the roots). If you find problems, test your soil for nematodes. No controls are available to consumers, but preplant solarization helps.

Scale insects are small pests that live on the stems of plants. Soon after hatching, they find a spot to settle down, insert their mouthparts into the plant, and suck sap. Over time, their legs atrophy, and a hard, waxy shell forms over their bodies. Several species attack ground covers. English ivy, wintercreeper, ferns, and pachysandra are among the ground covers affected. Apply horticultural oil to smother them, or use a systemic pesticide.

Spider mites are major garden pests that attack juniper, pachysandra, and other ground covers. They suck sap from the undersides of leaves, turning them a sickly yellowish-brown. Control spider mites with insecticidal soap.

Snails and slugs thrive in cool, damp spots, hiding under thick ground covers during the day and coming out to feed at night. They damage by chewing holes in leaves and are particularly fond of hosta, ginger, and phlox. Sprinkle granular bait containing metaldehyde, such as Bug-Geta, around plants to control slugs and snails. Wet down the area beforehand. You can also handpick the pests at night.

Many leaf spot diseases afflict ground covers. Most are fungal diseases that thrive in moist environments and mild temperatures. Spots may be irregular to circular brown, tan, or black. Some, such as those affecting lippia, are mainly unsightly. Others, such as bacterial leaf spot on ivy, kill plants over time. Take a sample of the problem to nursery or extension staff, who can identify the problem and recommend a solution.

Moles, gophers, deer, and other wildlife may be the hardest pests to control. Apply repellents, such as garlic and fungicides containing thiram. These require several applications because they wear off with time. They're not particularly effective. Or use a physical barrier, such as bird netting, to keep deer and rabbits from plants.

MAKING IT SAFER AND EASIER

As much fun as gardening is, it can be dangerous if you aren't careful when using tools and chemicals. Take precautions to protect yourself from injury. The following guidelines will make your work safer and some gardening tasks easier.

CLOTHING

First, wear appropriate clothes. Wear long pants to protect your legs from cuts and scrapes as well as from skin irritations caused by poisonous plants, insects, or chemicals.

Put on a cap or broad-brimmed hat to protect your face if you're spending a lot of time in the sun. Apply sunscreen, at least SPF 15, even on cloudy days.

Wear heavy shoes or boots, especially when using motorized equipment such as a rototiller or mower or when digging with a shovel. Heavy soles make it easier to push a shovel into the soil, and their thick uppers protect your toes and feet from injury should you slip. Don't disable safety shutoffs, even if they make equipment inconvenient to use.

Gloves are especially important when digging in rough soil or applying fertilizers, pesticides, or mulches that may contain irritating substances.

TECHNIQUES

When digging, especially if you are breaking new, tough ground, keep your back straight, your shoulders upright, and your knees bent. Don't slump or stoop.

Bending from the waist to weed or plant will strain your back. Instead, get some knee pads and kneel or squat as you work. But don't squat for extended periods of time to avoid muscle pulls and wear and tear on your knees and lower back. Rest on your knees and sit back on your feet if you need a break.

Work the ground when it is moist but not wet; wet soil is heavier and harder to lift than dry soil. Take small scoops with your shovel so you aren't straining to lift a heavy load. As you lift, grip the shovel close to the blade for better leverage. To protect your back and shoulders from injury as you lift the shovel or swing a hoe, do so in one fluid movement rather than in short jerks.

When using clippers or pruners, swap them from hand to hand to avoid a repetitive motion injury in your wrist or hands. Buy the best pruners you can afford. High-quality tools

Take care when filling the sprayer. Follow all clothing guidelines on the pesticide label, and wear chemical-resistant gloves. Don't overfill the sprayer.

will take the brunt of the force, rather than directing it to your hand, arm, and back.

WORKING WITH PESTICIDES AND FERTILIZER

When applying fertilizers or pesticides, follow the guidelines for clothing that are listed on the label. Usually that means wearing long pants and a long-sleeved shirt to keep any residue off your skin. Wear a lightweight dust mask to avoid breathing in airborne mist or dust. Some labels specify using a respirator.

The most dangerous time for handling a pesticide is while pouring it and mixing it in the sprayer. At this point you are working with undiluted material, so a small spill can be toxic. Any time you spill a chemical on your skin, wash the area immediately and thoroughly.

Your face and groin are the most vulnerable areas of your body. Avoid splashing chemicals on your clothing or skin in these areas. Always wash your hands thoroughly before eating, rubbing your eyes, or using the rest room.

As you mix the pesticide, wear chemical-resistant gloves to protect your hands from spills. Look for gloves made from neoprene rubber, which stands up to the solvents in many pesticides. Wash your hands and face thoroughly after applying chemicals. Wash clothing in a separate batch from other clothes.

Be smart when using pesticides. They are poisons, but they are safe to use as long as you use them correctly. Everything you need to know about using a product is on its label. Read it and follow all the guidelines it lays out.

PROPAGATION

Taking cuttings is an easy way to increase the ground covers in your landscape.

Even when you pay just a dollar each, buying plants to fill a large ground cover bed will put a dent in your pocketbook. One way around the expense is to propagate the plants yourself. Your friends' beds and other existing plantings are a good resource.

Many ground covers reproduce by seed, or you can use vegetative means—stem, leaf, or root cuttings, dividing, or layering—to propagate them. Plants propagated vegetatively are identical to the parent plant. Those arising from seed vary; they combine the traits of both the mother and father plant. Different species of plants require different means of propagation. You'll find the details for each ground cover in the Plant Selection Guide.

CUTTINGS

Growing plants from cuttings simply means removing a leaf or section of stem or root from a plant and placing it in a moist growing medium where it will form roots. Woody plants and vines propagate easily from stem cuttings, herbaceous plants and succulents from leaf and stem cuttings. Root cuttings work well for plants that grow from rhizomes.

The growing medium is critical to success. Water should quickly soak into it and drain out, yet the medium should remain moist. Most commercial potting soils meet these criteria, as do perlite and vermiculite, used singly or together. Half-and-half mixes of sand and peat moss or perlite and peat are fine, too. Garden soil is not; it is too dense in pots.

Time of year also affects success. Woody ground covers can be propagated from softwood cuttings (those taken in early summer before stems are hard and inflexible), semi-hardwood cuttings (in midsummer when stems are firming up), and hardwood cuttings (stems are stiff and woody). You can take hardwood cuttings from late fall through early spring, before plants begin growth.

Most woody plants root rapidly from tender, actively growing softwood or semi-

hardwood cuttings. Hardwood cuttings take longer to root than the other two, but for some plants, such as broadleaf evergreens, they produce healthier, more vigorous roots. Herbaceous ground covers always provide softwood cuttings.

Cuttings need humidity to root. After inserting them in the growing medium, seal them in a plastic bag. Once a day, loosen the bag to air it out or to water, then reseal.

The cuttings are ready to transplant when they show new growth or when tugged they "tug back," meaning they have roots. You can shift them to small pots to grow awhile longer or transplant them into the bed.

STEM CUTTINGS: The night before harvesting cuttings, water the ground cover bed well. Early the next morning, clip healthy side shoots that have no buds or flowers from plants. Use proper pruning techniques, cutting back to a node or main stem and leaving no stubs. With ground covers such as ivy, you can take one or two long shoots and slice them into several cuttings. Take random individual stems from shrubby ground covers.

Next, trim each cutting to 3 to 6 inches long, leaving at least three leaf nodes. Make a slanted cut at the top of the cutting and a straight cut at the bottom so you can tell the ends apart at planting. Remove leaves from the lower inch or two of the cutting. Dip the bottom end in a rooting hormone and insert it into the medium.

If you can't plant the cuttings immediately, store them in the refrigerator for several days. Maintain moderate temperatures; do not let the cuttings freeze.

Hardwood cuttings can be kept dormant until spring. Dip them in rooting hormone, then bundle them together. In areas where the ground freezes in winter, store them in a refrigerator or a cool basement until you can root them outdoors. In mild climates, bury the bundles in a shallow trench outdoors. As they lie dormant, the stems form calluses at the ends, where new growth will occur. When the weather warms up, transplant the cuttings to the ground cover bed or to large pots.

ROOT CUTTINGS: Take root cuttings in spring or fall, whenever you divide the plants. Any ground cover that sprouts from its roots can be propagated this way. Remove the parent plant from the soil. Snip off a root and cut it into sections about as long as a pencil is wide. Lay these sections flat on potting soil. Cover them with potting soil, or insert them in a soil-filled pot with their tops at soil level.

Moisten the soil and cover the pot with a plastic bag. Store it in a shady spot. Keep cuttings moist until you see new stem growth. Then transplant them into larger containers or directly into a bed.

DIVISION

You can divide any ground cover that grows from bulbs or rhizomes or that forms spreading clumps with multiple crowns, such as irises, daylilies, pachysandra, ajuga, and ornamental grasses. Not only does division provide you with new plants, it relieves overcrowding in the bed and helps tidy it up. Divide spring-blooming plants in late summer or early fall; divide summer-blooming plants in early spring.

Dig up the parent plant and look for the individual crowns. If the parent has fibrous roots, you can gently separate the crowns from the parent. Ground covers that form clumps or grow from bulbs, rhizomes, or tuberous roots can be broken apart, or sliced into pieces with a large knife or spade. Plant divided sections in the prepared beds.

LAYERING

Layering is slower than rooting plants from cuttings or dividing, but it is an easy way to start new plants. It works best with ground covers that root from their stems, such as barberry, heath, and ivy.

To layer, dig a shallow hole in the soil next to the parent ground cover. Select a flexible branch low on the plant. Cut halfway through it and insert a pebble in the cut. Gently anchor the stem in the hole with a metal staple or layering pin, with the pin between the parent and the cut. Stake the tip of the branch so that some leaves rise above the soil surface. Refill the hole and set a brick or rock on top.

Occasionally check for rooting (move the brick and scrape away the soil). Once roots are abundant and appear to be growing well, cut the "baby" from its parent and move it to a new site. Rooting may take a year, so be patient.

GROUND COVERS FROM SEED

You get a lot for little money when growing ground covers from seed, but it takes planning, because you must start them well in advance of installing the bed.

The easiest way to propagate from seed is to dig up volunteer seedlings from a ground cover bed. You can also collect seeds from the bed or buy them from nurseries.

Some ground covers, such as wintercreeper, can be seeded directly into the bed, either in spring after the chance for frost has passed or in fall well before winter. Others need to be started indoors.

Most ground cover species vary in the amount of time it takes from sowing to transplanting, depth of planting, spacing,

Layering lets you propagate plants without disturbing the parent plant. Cut partway through the stem (inset), then pin the cut area to the ground. Cover it with soil. Roots will form at the cut and produce a new plant.

the need for any kind of special treatment, and so on. Check with the nursery supplying the seed or an extension agent for details.

Fill flats or pots with potting mix, sow the seeds, then water thoroughly with a fine mist. Move the flats under grow lights.

As the seeds germinate, keep the soil moist but not wet, and occasionally rotate the flats so they receive uniform light. If the seedlings grow tall and spindly, they are reaching for light and their stems will be weak. Lower the lights to about 2 inches above the surface of the flat. As the plants grow taller, gradually raise the lights. If the seedlings look brown or burned, they may be getting too much light. Raise the lights or move the flats to a spot with less direct light.

Keep seedlings damp and warm until they are ready to transplant; they will have developed their first set of true leaves, which look like the leaves of a mature plant, as opposed to the initial seed leaves. If you can't plant the seedlings immediately after they have developed true leaves, transplant them to pots and give them plenty of space to grow.

Harden off the seedlings before planting them in a bed. This acclimates seedlings from their relatively stable and pampered indoor growing conditions to more variable and severe outdoor conditions. Take flats outdoors on mild days for a few hours each day, and gradually lengthen the time over a week. If frost is predicted, bring the flats inside or cover them. Cutting back on water also helps harden off plants, but water them thoroughly at planting time.

Choosing the right plants for your setting and environment is the best way to ensure that ground covers work well. Use this plant guide to make the proper selection.

PLANT SELECTION GUIDE

If variety is the spice of life, you'll be thrilled with the diversity of ground covers that can spice up your landscape. In this chapter you will become familiar with nearly 200 of them. They are the most commonly used ground covers and should be readily available from local nurseries and mail-order sources—possibly even from your neighbors and friends.

Here's how to use this guide.

FAST FACTS

The plants in this selection guide are listed in alphabetical order by their botanical names, with their common names highlighted. Individual listings for ferns, heaths and heathers, ornamental grasses, shrubby ground cover cultivars, and vines are grouped together under their respective headings.

Each entry offers a quick reference of basic details about each plant, including its hardiness, type (evergreen, deciduous, shrub, perennial, and so on), and approximate height at maturity. Most plants in this encyclopedia are adapted to a range of hardiness zones. To determine which zone you live in, refer to the Hardiness Zone Map on page 96.

We define ground covers as plants that grow no more than 3 feet high; however, some of the plants listed here, especially vines and shrubs, are capable of growing much taller than that unless they are pruned or trained to trail on the ground or unless you select a low-growing variety. The description of each plant lets you know if it requires additional maintenance as a ground cover.

Also included in the thumbnail list of plant information is the plant spacing for each ground cover based on its spread and growth rate. You'll also find the required exposure, which tells you whether the plant is suited for shade or sun or can be used in a variety of lighting situations.

Finally, the list offers the plant's water needs, the amount of water the ground cover requires once it is established. Keep in mind that plants need more water as they are becoming established, and their need for water may vary with weather conditions. Water needs are categorized as "low," meaning that established plants can go for extended periods of time without watering; "moderate," meaning that plants can tolerate drying out between waterings but must have an occasional watering to keep from wilting, especially during hot, dry weather; and "frequent," meaning that plants require constant moisture in their root zones and will not tolerate drying out.

DESCRIPTIONS

The list of fast facts is followed by a detailed plant description, which includes the plant's leaf and stem structure, its spread and height at maturity, and the color of its foliage, flowers, and fruit. Photographs accompany each entry to help you visualize how these plants might look in your landscape. A section on care tells you briefly how to propagate, fertilize, and maintain these plants, and sometimes includes typical problems the plant has. Finally, a section on uses gives you ideas for situations in which the plant is especially appropriate.

YOUR OWN LIST

Leaf through these pages and list plants that interest you. Use your list to check with local gardeners, extension specialists, landscape designers, and nurseries to determine which ground covers are best suited for your situation and are available in your area. If you find yourself drawn to a plant that is not commonly used in your area but still meets your cultural requirements, get a few and try them in a small planting. You may be pleasantly surprised.

ACHILLEA
Yarrow

This woolly yarrow has more delicate, feathery foliage than Greek or silvery yarrow.

- Hardy in Zones 3 to 10
- Evergreen perennial
- 4 to 10 inches tall
- Space 12 to 18 inches
- Full sun
- Moderate watering

DESCRIPTION: These undemanding plants have gray to green, aromatic, fernlike leaves. Foliage forms 4- to 10-inch-tall mats that spread 1 to 3 feet. Tiny flowers of white, cream, pink, or yellow on large, flat-headed clusters rise to 10 inches above the foliage and bloom spring to fall. Yarrow prefers fertile, moist soil but does fine in any well-drained soil.

Greek yarrow (*A. ageratifolia*) has silvery, lobed or smooth-edged leaves and white flowers. Silvery yarrow (*A. clavennae*) has silver-gray, lobed leaves and ivory flowers. Woolly yarrow (*A. tomentosa*) grows 3 to 12 inches high with feathery, gray-green leaves and sulfur yellow flowers.

CARE INSTRUCTIONS: Cut faded flowers for longer bloom and neat appearance. Divide crowded plants every two to three years. Plants may need more frequent watering in arid regions; overwatering may lead to mildew. Propagate from seed, division, or cuttings. Problems: crown gall; powdery mildew; stem rot; rust.

USES: Areas with light foot traffic.

AEGOPODIUM PODAGRARIA
Goutweed

Goutweed makes a fine edging plant. It is a mint relative and can spread rapidly.

- Hardy in Zones 3 to 9
- Deciduous perennial
- 6 to 14 inches tall
- Space 12 inches
- Sun to shade
- Moderate watering

DESCRIPTION: Fragrant, slender, light green leaves form a dense, creeping foliage mass that rises to about 6 inches high. Small clusters of flowers rise 14 inches on slender stems in summer. 'Variegatum' displays light green leaves with silvery-white margins.

Adaptable to many soil types, goutweed does fine with limited water but doesn't like soggy soil. In fertile soil with regular watering, it may be invasive. 'Variegatum' grows more slowly than other varieties and is less likely to become invasive.

CARE INSTRUCTIONS: Mow two or three times each growing season for neat appearance. Install a barrier buried in the soil around the growing area's margins to keep plants in check. Deadhead flowers to prevent reseeding. May be divided in spring or fall. Propagate from seed, cuttings, or division.

USES: Between barriers, such as a house and a sidewalk; edging walkways.

AGAPANTHUS
African Lily

African lilies mix well with a lower-growing ground cover.

- Hardy in Zones 9 and 10
- Evergreen to deciduous bulb
- 1 to 2 feet tall
- Space 18 to 24 inches
- Sun to light shade
- Frequent watering

DESCRIPTION: African lilies grow in a fountain-like clump of shiny, long leaves. White to dark blue flowers are borne above the foliage on sturdy stems from early spring to early fall. Each cluster of flowers can contain 100 blossoms, which open successively 20 or so at a time. Plants grow quickly, but the clumps do not spread rapidly. The foliage is persistent, although it may die back during winter or dry weather.

'Peter Pan' is 12 inches tall with blue blossoms on 12- to 18-inch stems. 'Albus' has white flowers. 'Rancho White' (also sold as 'Dwarf White' and 'Rancho') forms 18-inch-tall clumps and has white flowers on 2-foot-tall stems.

African lily prefers partial to full sun and moist, fertile soil, but can do well in poorer soils if fertilized and watered regularly.

CARE INSTRUCTIONS: Divide occasionally when beds become crowded, about every four to five years. Propagate from seed or division. Problems: slugs, snails.

USES: Interplanted with lower-growing ground covers.

AJUGA

Ajuga

- Hardy in Zones 4 to 10
- Semi-evergreen to evergreen herbaceous perennial
- 4 to 9 inches tall
- Space 6 to 18 inches
- Sun to shade
- Moderate to frequent watering

DESCRIPTION: Glossy, spoon-shaped leaves grow in a low rosette; leaf colors range from dark green to tinged with bronze, white, pink, or purple. Some species and cultivars have larger leaves and taller flower spikes. Leaves grow larger in shade.

Blue to lavender and sometimes pink and white flowers appear in spring and early summer on 6- to 9-inch-tall spikes.

Bugleweed (*A. pyramidalis*) forms a 6-inch-tall mat; carpet bugle (*A. reptans*) grows to 4 inches. Ajuga grows best in sun or partial shade and in well-drained, sandy loam. It tolerates heavy soil.

CARE INSTRUCTIONS: Mow after flowering; divide when vigor declines or bare spots appear. Fertilize annually. Propagate by division or cuttings. Problems: root rot or fungus in wet soils and dense plantings; crown rot; mosaic virus; aphids.

USES: Border edging; beneath shrubs and hardy perennials; mass plantings to cover small to medium-size areas; in shade as lawn alternative.

Ajuga comes in many foliage colors, from green to the reddish tinge of this 'Burgundy Glow'.

ARABIS

Rockcress

- Hardy in Zones 5 to 9
- Woody evergreen perennial
- 6 to 12 inches tall
- Space 8 to 12 inches
- Sun to light shade
- Moderate watering

DESCRIPTION: Several *Arabis* species make fine ground covers in cool regions. Wallcress (*A. caucasica*) has been in the trade for years; rockcress (*A. procurrens*) is a relative newcomer. Both have gray-green, mat-forming foliage and white fragrant flowers in early

spring. Wallcress grows 6 to 12 inches tall, rockcress 12 inches tall.

Cultivars include 'Flore Plena', double white flowers; 'Spring Charm', roselike blooms; 'Variegata', white flowers and creamy white margins on gray leaves; 'Pink Pearl', deep pink blossoms.

Both species prefer sandy, well-drained soil. In dry regions, rockcress prefers light shade.

CARE INSTRUCTIONS: Shear or mow after blooming to improve appearance. Refresh plantings with new plants or rooted cuttings when beds grow bare or ragged. Propagate by seed, cuttings, or division. Problems: clubroot; downy mildew; leaf spot; white rust; lily aphids.

USES: Small areas; as cover for bulb beds or rock gardens.

Rockcress is ideal for rock gardens and as a cover for bulb beds.

ARCTOSTAPHYLOS

Manzanita and Bearberry

- Hardiness varies
- Evergreen shrubs
- 1 inch to 24 inches tall
- Space 12 to 48 inches
- Sun to partial shade
- Moderate watering

DESCRIPTION: All plants in this genus have evergreen leaves, urn- or bell-shaped flowers, showy fruit, and purple bark. They are drought- and salt-tolerant plants, forming dense

mats across an area. Plants root at the stems.

Bearberry (*A. uva-ursi*), also called creeping manzanita, is hardy in Zones 3 to 10 on the West Coast, Zones 3 to 7 in the East. Slow to establish and easy to maintain, it has dense coverage. Its dark green, leathery foliage turns bronze in winter. Waxy, pink spring flowers are followed by long-lasting red fruit. Little Sur manzanita (*A. edmundsii*) grows in Zones 8 to 10, reaching to 12 inches tall with light green leaves and pink flowers in winter. Both plants prefer well-drained acid to neutral soil.

CARE INSTRUCTIONS: Mulch new plants. Water thoroughly and frequently, then once or twice a

month; avoid overwatering. Prune in spring. Propagate from seed or cuttings. Problems: root rot; black mildew; leaf gall; leaf spot; rust.

USES: Hillsides in coastal or dry regions.

Bearberry is an ideal choice for dry and coastal regions.

ARENARIA

Sandwort

Corsican sandwort can be used as a lawn substitute.

- Hardy in Zones 3 to 10
- Semi-evergreen to evergreen perennial
- 3 to 8 inches tall
- Space 12 to 16 inches
- Partial shade to full sun
- Frequent watering

DESCRIPTION: Sandworts have a low-growing or matting habit that forms a lush carpet. Most common are Corsican sandwort (*A. balearica*) and Irish moss (*A. verna*, also known as *Minuartia verna*). Both tolerate foot traffic. Corsican sandwort has small, thick, glossy green leaves and small, white, round flowers in midspring. It can be grown in shade. Irish moss has narrow, grasslike, light green leaves and star-shaped, white flowers in midspring. Sandworts prefer good-quality, sandy, well-drained soil.

CARE INSTRUCTIONS: Cut plants into small squares and plant at or slightly below soil surface. If plants begin to form humps as they mature, cut away small strips from the edges and press back down to soil level. In colder climates, mulch plants in winter. Propagate by seed or division.

USES: Lawn alternative in small areas; between stepping-stones and pavers.

ARMERIA MARITIMA

Thrift

Thrift forms banks of foliage and flowers that can be useful in almost any setting.

- Hardy in Zones 3 to 10
- Evergreen perennial
- 3 to 6 inches tall
- Space 6 to 12 inches
- Sun to light shade
- Moderate watering

DESCRIPTION: Thrift has soft, fine-textured leaves that grow in a grasslike mound that is about 6 inches tall and about a foot wide. Its tight, 1-inch, round clusters of pink or white flowers rise 6 to 12 inches above the foliage on strong, slender stems. Flowers appear in spring in cold climates and almost year-round in mild climates.

Thrift grows best in well-drained soil of average fertility. Soil that's too moist around roots or overly fertile result in the plants dying out in the center of the clump.

CARE INSTRUCTIONS: After blooming has ceased, deadhead spent flowers to keep a well-groomed appearance. Water plants growing in well-drained soil regularly. However, plants will survive with relatively little irrigation. In heavy soil that holds water, avoid overwatering to keep problems with root rot at bay, or amend soil to improve drainage. Propagate by division.

USES: Seaside gardens; rock gardens; between stepping-stones; useful in almost any setting.

ARTEMISIA

Artemisia

Artemisias such as this 'Silver Mound' take to hot, dry, sunny sites. They're good next to paving.

- Hardy in Zones 5 to 9
- Evergreen perennial
- Up to 2 feet tall
- Space 1 to 2 feet
- Sun
- Low to moderate watering

DESCRIPTION: These hardy, shrubby or herbaceous plants are members of the daisy family. Some are grown for their ornamental, fragrant leaves, others for their flowers. 'Silver Mound' (*A. schmidtiana*) forms silvery, fine-textured, 12-inch-tall mounds. It grows best in well-drained, infertile soil, becoming floppy in rich soil. Roman wormwood (*A. pontica*) has feathery leaves that are whitish or ash gray underneath and fragrant when crushed. Its creamy white flowers bloom in September. Some artemisias are used as herbs. Soft, gray-green leaves look silky and produce dense, spreading coverage. Small, insignificant yellow flowers appear within foliage in summer. Artemisias grow best in well-drained soil and full sun.

CARE INSTRUCTIONS: Water in dry weather. Propagate shrubby artemisia from cuttings taken in August or September. Perennial types can be propagated by division. Divide plants in spring before new growth appears.

USES: Hard-to-water or drought areas; good as firebreaks.

ASARUM

Wild Ginger

- Hardy in Zones 5 to 9 (West, except desert)
- Evergreen perennial
- 10 inches tall
- Space 12 inches
- Full shade
- Frequent watering

DESCRIPTION: All species form a dense, coarse-textured cover of dark green, heart-shaped leaves. European wild ginger (*A. europaeum*) has shiny leaves. Canadian wild ginger (*A. canadense*) has larger and slightly hairy leaves; it is also more heat-tolerant than European wild ginger. British Columbia ginger (*A. caudatum*) is similar. Numerous cultivars of shuttleworth ginger (*A. shuttleworthii*) with beautiful silvery variegation are available (this species is hardy only to Zone 7).

Wild gingers have unusual, reddish flowers in spring, usually hidden under the foliage. All need shade and moisture to thrive. They prefer rich, moisture-retaining soil, but can grow in well-drained soil if watered frequently.

CARE INSTRUCTIONS: Protect from drying winds and water well; fertilize once a year. Propagate by division. Problems: slugs, snails.

USES: Woodland settings; interplanted with evergreen shrubs and wildflowers.

Few ground covers beat wild ginger in shade gardens or interplanted with shrubs and wildflowers.

ASPIDISTRA ELATIOR

Cast-Iron Plant

- Hardy in Zones 8 to 10
- Evergreen perennial
- Up to 2 feet tall
- Space 2 feet
- Light to full shade
- Moderate watering

DESCRIPTION: This tough plant requires little attention to thrive. Its large, broad, dark green leaves grow in patches. Large, well-established plants occasionally produce purplish brown flowers that develop inconspicuously among leaves or underground. Leaves grow on stout stems and have prominent veins. 'Variegata' has dark green leaves with white veins.

Cast-iron plant tolerates deep shade better than many other plants. It endures poor soil, drought, and neglect but prefers rich, porous soil.

CARE INSTRUCTIONS: Water when soil is fairly dry. Remove dead or bleached leaves. Fertilize moderately to enhance leaf growth. Propagate by division.

USES: In deep shade and as border plants; good underplanting for azaleas and camellias.

Cast-iron plant is aptly named; it is practically invincible.

ASTILBE CHINENSIS

Chinese Astilbe

- Hardy in Zones 4 to 8
- Deciduous perennial
- 4 to 10 inches tall
- Space 6 to 18 inches
- Sun to partial shade
- Moderate to frequent watering

DESCRIPTION: The fernlike, dark green to bronze leaves of Chinese astilbe form low mats. Clusters of pink flowers on 1-foot stems rise above the foliage in summer.

Plants do well in soggy places and near pools or ponds. If left undisturbed, they form large, free-blooming stands. Chinese astilbe is easy to grow. It spreads slowly; for faster coverage, use the 6-inch spacing.

CARE INSTRUCTIONS: Keep moist and water frequently if planted in a sunny location. Provide fertile, moist soil amended with organic matter. Propagate by division in spring or from seed. Divide plants every few years if they become overcrowded.

USES: Woodland settings; shady, moist places where other plants will not grow; interplanted with other shade plants.

The pink blooms on Chinese astilbe last about four weeks. The foliage is attractive on its own.

Basket-of-gold brings bright color to the landscape and works well tumbling from crevices in rock walls and gardens.

AURINIA SAXATILIS
Basket-of-Gold

- Hardy in Zones 4 to 10
- Deciduous to evergreen perennial
- Up to 6 inches tall
- Space 10 to 12 inches
- Full sun
- Moderate watering

DESCRIPTION: This plant has small gray-green leaves 2 to 5 inches long and vivid yellow-gold flowers in spring.

Basket-of-gold thrives in full sun and well-drained soil. The appearance of the plant varies depending on where it is grown. In rich, moist soil, it tends to open and sprawling; in dry, poor soil, the plant is compact and bushy. Basket-of-gold is fairly short-lived, but it self-sows freely once established.

CARE INSTRUCTIONS: Cut back stems after flowering to stimulate growth. Easily propagated from seed and by division.

USES: Rock gardens; crevices of rock walls; as mass plantings.

BACCHARIS PILULARIS
Coyote Brush

Coyote brush is a hardy ground cover ideal for salty, dry regions.

- Hardy in Zones 8 to 10 (West)
- Woody shrub
- 8 to 24 inches, depending on species
- Space 2 to 3 feet
- Sun to light shade
- Low to moderate watering

DESCRIPTION: This mounded shrub grows up to 2 feet tall and spreads 6 feet or more. It has small white flowers that are often hard to see. Green, glossy leaves densely cover its branches.

Buy plants propagated from seedless male plants. Female plants have plumelike, cottony seed heads that can be messy.

Coyote brush does well in many soil types and climates, although it is best adapted to the western United States. It prefers well-drained soil but can thrive in damp, foggy climates in sandy soil or in heavier or alkaline soil and desert heat.

CARE INSTRUCTIONS: Water occasionally; regular watering is required only during extremely hot and dry summers. Prune old, woody branches and leggy, upright stems in late fall. Propagate from young stem cuttings in late summer or from seed.

USES: Southwestern gardens; drought areas.

BERGENIA
Bergenia

Bergenias do especially well in damp areas around pools and streams.

- Hardy in Zones 3 to 10 (except desert)
- Evergreen perennial
- 18 to 24 inches tall
- Space 18 inches
- Sun to partial shade
- Moderate to frequent watering

DESCRIPTION: Bergenias form clumps of broad, rounded, rubbery-looking glossy leaves on short stalks. They spread 20 to 24 inches. Heart-leaf bergenia (*B. cordifolia*) has 10-inch-long leaves with wavy edges and heart-shaped bases. The dark green leaves have a purple tinge. Pink flower clusters bloom on red stems from winter to spring; some are hidden by foliage. Leather bergenia (*B. crassifolia*) blooms in winter with pink, lilac, or purple flowers that rise above the foliage. It has broad, oval, 8-inch leaves with wavy margins. The heart-shaped leaves of fringed bergenia (*B. ciliata*) are dark green, turning red in fall. Small, cup-shaped white or pink-tinged flowers appear early spring.

Bergenias like good soil and plenty of water but tolerate poorer soil and less water in cool regions.

CARE INSTRUCTIONS: Shelter from wind. Divide rootstocks when humps form. Collect seeds. Remove dead leaves annually. Problems: slugs, snails.

USES: Around pools and streams; among rocks.

BOUGAINVILLEA SPECTABILIS

Bougainvillea

- Hardy in Zones 10 and 11
- Woody deciduous to evergreen vine
- 1 to 2 feet tall
- Space 6 to 8 feet
- Sun to light shade
- Moderate to frequent watering

DESCRIPTION: Bougainvillea has a trailing habit, which is typically trained to climb walls or arbors. Dark green leaves are oval to heart-shaped. The sprawling stems are thorny. Showy "flowers" (actually bracts) appear in spring and summer in a wide range of colors including pink, violet, purple, red, yellow, bronze, orange, white, and multicolor combinations.

Plants need minimum winter temperature of 55° F. They grow rampantly; may become invasive. **CARE INSTRUCTIONS:** Water regularly; reduce watering in midsummer to increase blooming and to keep plants in bounds. Fertilize in midsummer and again in fall. Train or prune to trail; if upright stems cannot be trained to lie close to the ground, prune them to 1 inch long in spring, leaving two lateral buds at the base in February. Propagate from semi-hardwood cuttings in summer. Roots are fragile, so take care at planting. Problems: whiteflies, mealybugs. **USES:** On slopes; trailing over walls; as barrier.

Pruning keeps this bougainvillea looking neat, but it can also be lovely if allowed to ramble.

CAMPANULA

Bellflower

- Hardy in Zones 4 to 10 (West), 4 to 9 (East)
- Evergreen perennial
- 12 inches tall
- Space 12 inches
- Sun to light shade
- Moderate to frequent watering

DESCRIPTION: *Campanula* includes 300 species that vary in size and growth habit. Ground cover species include Dalmatian bellflower (*C. portenschlagiana* or *C. muralis*) and Serbian bellflower (*C. poscharskyana*). Dalmatian bellflower grows 4 to 7 inches tall, with nearly round, wavy leaves on long stalks. Bell-shaped, bright blue to violet flowers cover foliage from midspring to summer. Serbian bellflower has a trailing habit and light green, medium-size, heart-shaped leaves. Star-shaped blue to lavender blooms appear in midspring through early summer. Stems may reach 12 inches.

Plants prefer good-quality, well-drained soil. They grow best in sunny spots in cooler regions; need some shade in warmer climates. **CARE INSTRUCTIONS:** Water regularly; Serbian bellflower can withstand less frequent watering. Deadhead flowers to prolong bloom. Propagate by seed or division in fall or spring. Problems: slugs, snails. **USES:** Rock gardens; flower borders; woodland settings.

Dalmation bellflower is one of many ground cover campanulas.

CARISSA MACROCARPA

Natal Plum

- Hardy in Zones 9 to 10
- Evergreen shrub
- Up to 2 feet tall
- Space 6 feet
- Sun to light shade
- Moderate watering

DESCRIPTION: Natal plum has dark green, shiny leaves and fragrant white or pink flowers, which are sometimes followed by edible, scarlet-colored, plumlike fruits. Sharp spines make natal plum an excellent barrier plant.

Most natal plums grow 6 feet tall, but several cultivars have a pro-strate—ground-hugging—habit and make fine ground covers. These include 'Horizontalis', which grows to about 2 feet; 'Green Carpet', which reaches about 1½ feet; and 'Prostrata', which also grows to about 2 feet. 'Tuttlei' grows 3 feet tall and has a semi-prostrate habit.

This versatile plant adapts to almost any setting. It grows well in any soil but prefers well-drained soil and bright sun. Plants do well in coastal areas. **CARE INSTRUCTIONS:** Propagate from seed and cuttings. **USES:** Coastal areas; barrier plant.

'Tuttlei' is one of the taller natal plums. All are versatile plants that direct traffic well.

CERASTIUM TOMENTOSUM

Snow-in-Summer

Bright white flowers make snow-in-summer a sparkling addition to the spring and summer landscape.

■ Hardy in Zones 3 to 10
■ Evergreen perennial
■ 4 to 10 inches tall
■ Space 12 to 18 inches
■ Sun
■ Moderate watering

DESCRIPTION: Woolly, narrow, silvery gray to white leaves are less than 1 inch long and grow in a matting habit. Short stems bear masses of small, snowy white flowers that cover the plant from late spring into summer.

The plant does well in many climates, from cool coastal areas to desert regions. It prefers well-drained, sandy soil; in hot regions, it may need partial shade.

Snow-in-summer will thrive with frequent watering but is susceptible to root rot, so don't allow it to stay wet for prolonged periods. It is a short-lived plant and may have to be refreshed with divisions or cuttings after a few years.

CARE INSTRUCTIONS: Shear off flower stems or mow after blooming has ceased. Be careful not to pair it with more delicate plants, as it can be aggressive and may overrun its neighbors.

USES: Rock gardens; steep banks; coastal or desert areas.

CERATOSTIGMA PLUMBAGINOIDES

Plumbago

Fast-growing plumbago brings color to the landscape in late summer and early fall.

■ Hardy in Zones 6 to 10 (except desert)
■ Deciduous to semi-evergreen perennial
■ 6 to 12 inches tall
■ Space 12 to 18 inches
■ Sun to light shade
■ Moderate watering

DESCRIPTION: Fast-spreading, long-stemmed plants have oval leaves and wiry, zigzagging stems. Leathery leaves are dark green to bronze-green, turning bronze-red in late fall. Clusters of cobalt blue flowers bloom from midsummer to midfall. Plants spread underground rapidly and form a dense mat.

Plumbago thrives in well-drained, good-quality soil but will tolerate a wide range of soil types from clay to sand. It grows only in mild climates. Wet soil does not promote growth. Plants spread rapidly in light soil.

CARE INSTRUCTIONS: Prune old flowering growth in spring; shear or mow plants after flowering, before new growth begins. Thin plants in spring if crowded and bare spots appear. Propagate by division in spring or from cuttings taken in summer. Mulch plants in winter in Zones 5 to 7.

USES: Rock gardens; late-summer color.

Chamomile is a good lawn substitute that releases a lovely fragrance when crushed underfoot.

CHAMAEMELUM NOBILE

Chamomile

■ Hardy in Zones 4 to 10
■ Evergreen perennial
■ 4 to 12 inches tall
■ Space 12 inches
■ Sun
■ Low to moderate watering

DESCRIPTION: This fragrant (apple-scented) perennial herb has lacy, finely divided leaves and small, daisylike white flowers. It grows in a flat mat against the soil and tolerates foot traffic well, releasing a lovely aroma when crushed underfoot. Chamomile is a wonderful lawn alternative. You can make chamomile tea from its flowers. 'Flore Pleno' is a double-flowered form.

A sunny location with well-drained, slightly acid, sandy soil is best, but chamomile also tolerates heavy soil.

CARE INSTRUCTIONS: Trim in spring or mow to a height of 3 to 4 inches after flowering, particularly if used as a lawn alternative. Propagate from seed, cuttings, or division in early spring.

USES: Between stepping-stones and pavers; as a lawn alternative; in bulb beds.

CISTUS

Rock Rose

- Hardy in Zones 8 to 10
- Woody evergreen shrub
- Up to 3 feet tall
- Space 3 feet
- Full sun to partial shade
- Low to moderate watering

DESCRIPTION: Rock rose forms mounds of silvery gray foliage. Its lovely, roselike flowers are short-lived but continue to appear over a long period. A few rock roses grow quite large, so check labels carefully. White rock rose (C. × corbariensis) grows to 3 feet; sage rock rose (C. salviifolius) is only 2½ feet tall. 'Anne Palmer' is a prostrate hybrid with pink flowers that fade to white. 'Carl English' is 18 inches tall and 18 inches wide with soft pink blooms all summer. 'Brilliancy' has early magenta flowers and grows 2 to 3 feet tall by 6 to 8 feet wide.

All need a sunny location in light, well-drained soil.

CARE INSTRUCTIONS: Choose sites carefully; rock roses don't like to be disturbed. Prune only dead wood from mature plants; pinch back younger plants to encourage bushy growth. Propagate from seed in April or stem cuttings in summer.

USES: Hot, dry settings; coastal areas; hillsides and slopes.

Rock rose's charming flowers and silvery foliage are well-suited to a dry, hot setting.

CONVALLARIA MAJALIS

Lily-of-the-Valley

- Hardy in Zones 3 to 9 (except desert)
- Deciduous perennial
- 6 inches tall
- Space 6 to 12 inches
- Partial to deep shade
- Moderate to frequent watering

DESCRIPTION: This dense, fragrant ground cover has stalks of sweet-scented bell-shaped flowers with scalloped edges in spring. Most plants have snow-white flowers, but some cultivars have double or pink blooms. Some varieties have variegated leaves. Fruit is poisonous.

Lily-of-the-valley thrives and spreads rapidly in moist soil. In dry soil, it survives quite well, but it does not spread. Heat also slows the spread of the plants.

CARE INSTRUCTIONS: Water well throughout the year; fertilize in fall after first frost. In colder regions, protect plants from severe winter weather by covering beds with mulch in fall. Propagate lily-of-the-valley by division in fall.

USES: Woodlands; under trees and shrubs.

Lily-of-the-valley provides a dense ground cover for woodland settings.

CONVOLVULUS

Ground Morning Glory

- Hardy in Zones 8 to 10
- Climbing, rambling shrub
- Up to 2 feet tall
- Space 3 feet
- Full sun to light shade
- Low to moderate watering

DESCRIPTION: Heart-shaped leaves may be silvery or green. Funnel-shaped flowers are pink, lavender, and white in spring and summer. Some species are trailing plants; others are low-growing shrubs. Plants spread rapidly and can crowd neighbors or become invasive. Bush morning glories (C. cneorum and C. mauritanicus) are low-mounding species with white and purple flowers, respectively.

Plant grows in any regular, well-drained garden soil; prefers light, sandy soil and full sun. Best in desert environments, where it is less likely to become invasive.

CARE INSTRUCTIONS: Pinch shoot tips in summer to keep plant bushy. Propagate from seed or rooted cuttings in spring. Problems: iron chlorosis; spider mites.

USES: Rock gardens; desert settings.

Ground morning glories are well-adapted to desert landscapes.

CORNUS CANADENSIS

Bunchberry

Bunchberries provide beautiful foliage, flowers, and edible berries.

- Hardy in Zones 3 to 6
- Deciduous perennial
- 6 to 9 inches tall
- Space 6 to 12 inches
- Partial sun to shade
- Moderate to frequent watering

DESCRIPTION: This herbaceous perennial has creeping, woody roots. Its leaves radiate around the stems in whorls. As is typical of its dogwood cousins, bunchberry has small flowers surrounded by four to six showy white bracts in spring. After flowering, small bunches of bright red, edible fruits appear in late summer. Foliage turns bright yellow to red in autumn.

Bunchberry spreads by underground runners, but not invasively so. Plants can be difficult to establish; site preparation is the key to success. They prefer loose, moist, acid soil with plenty of organic matter mixed in.

CARE INSTRUCTIONS: Protect plants from strong winds. Hard pruning may be needed to prevent overgrowth. Propagate from seed or hardwood cuttings, or by layering in the fall.

USES: Mass planting; to attract wildlife.

COTONEASTER

Cotoneasters

Bearberry cotoneaster is a low-growing evergreen shrub.

Rock cotoneaster has a horizontal growth habit that can reach heights of 2 to 3 feet.

- Hardy in Zones 5 to 6
- Woody evergreen to deciduous shrub
- 1½ to 3 feet tall
- Space 3 to 5 feet
- Sun to partial shade
- Low to moderate watering

DESCRIPTION: These extremely versatile ground-cover plants range from low-growing mats to small trees. Most are deciduous; some are evergreen. Leaf color ranges from dark green to blue green. Some varieties grow best in sun, others in shade. Cotoneasters are valued for their dazzling autumn colors and vivid berries. Some produce white or pink-tinted flowers in early summer. None have showy flowers.

Good deciduous ground-cover choices abound. Cranberry cotoneaster (*C. apiculatus*) is the most cold-hardy species. It grows 3 feet tall and 3 to 6 feet across and is hardy to Zone 5. Cultivars include 'Nana', a dwarf form that is 12 inches tall and 4 feet wide.

Species hardy to Zone 6 include rockspray cotoneaster (*C. horizontalis*), which is 2 to 3 feet tall by 5 to 8 feet wide. The leaves of 'Variegatus' are marked with white along their edges. It is slow-growing and has rose-red fall color. The variety perpusillus (*C. h. perpusillus*) is more cold hardy (to Zone 5) and more prostrate. It grows 1 to 2 feet tall and 7 feet wide and has brilliant red fall color and fruit.

Creeping cotoneaster (*C. adpressus*), which grows about 1 foot tall by 4 to 6 feet across, is also hardy to Zone 6. Early cotoneaster (*C. nanshan*), once considered a variety of creeping cotoneaster and sometimes still listed as *C. adpressus* var. *praecox*, is about 18 inches tall and 6 feet wide. Its fruit is among the largest of the species.

Bearberry cotoneaster (*C. dammeri*) is an evergreen species that reaches 6 to 12 inches tall. It is hardy to Zone 6. 'Mooncreeper' is a 4-inch-tall cultivar; 'Coral Beauty' grows 2 feet tall by 6 feet wide and has coral-red berries. Many other cotoneaster species adapted to different regions and growing conditions are available.

Cotoneasters are easy to grow and tolerate air pollution. They grow in almost any soil and in sun or partial shade, but they prefer moist, well-drained soil and a sunny location. Many varieties don't do well in extremely hot or dry climates.

CARE INSTRUCTIONS: Prune only to remove dead twigs and straggling shoots. Older, overgrown shrubs may be cut back hard in early spring. Propagate from seed in late autumn or from stem cuttings of current-year growth in August or September. Problems: spider mites; fire blight.

USES: Banks and slopes; along walls; near buildings; dry settings.

CYTISUS

Broom

- Hardy in Zones 6 to 8
- Woody deciduous to evergreen shrub
- 2 feet tall
- Space 2 feet
- Full sun
- Low to moderate watering

DESCRIPTION: *Cytisus* encompasses 50 deciduous and evergreen shrubs, ranging from prostrate mats to erect shrubs. All have whiplike branches and deep green branchlets with few leaves. Pealike flowers are usually yellow but vary from white to cream to purple-tinged to crimson. They last from spring to early summer. Ground-cover brooms include prostrate broom (*C. decumbens*) and kew broom (*C. × kewensis*).

Brooms tolerate a variety of soils, either slightly acid or alkaline, as long as they are well-drained; they prefer dry, poor soil. They withstand hot weather.

CARE INSTRUCTIONS: Select site carefully; brooms don't tolerate transplanting. Shelter from strong winds. Pinch back new shoots each year to encourage bushy growth. Pinching is sufficient pruning for most species; a few species may benefit from a hard pruning every few years. Propagate from seed or semi-hardwood cuttings.

USES: Rock gardens; sunny borders; beds.

The broom group of plants offers many species in a wide range of sizes and growth habits.

DALEA GREGGII

Trailing Indigo Bush

- Hardy in Zones 9 and 10 (desert only)
- Evergreen woody shrub
- 1 foot tall
- Space 2 feet
- Sun
- Low to moderate watering

DESCRIPTION: The plant's low, spreading branches typically reach 1 foot in height but occasionally grow as high as 2 feet; plants spread 4 to 8 feet wide. Leaves are small, gray, and evergreen. Clusters of small lavender flowers appear from spring to early summer.

This desert plant is native to dry areas of the Western Hemisphere. It tolerates dry, hot climates and a wide range of soils if well-drained.

CARE INSTRUCTIONS: Tolerates drought, but watering deeply once a week will increase growth rate. Propagate from stem cuttings. Problem: Young plants and cuttings may succumb to an unidentified fungal pathogen.

USES: Desert regions; moderate to large areas; erosion control on level or sloping sites.

Trailing indigo bush is an ideal plant to add color and life to desert landscapes.

DELOSPERMA

Ice Plant

- Hardy in Zones 6 to 10
- Succulent perennial
- 3 to 4 inches tall
- Space 4 to 6 inches
- Sun to light shade
- Low watering

DESCRIPTION: This species of ice plant is similar to *Lampranthus*, but lower-growing. The name ice plant came about because the foliage is actually cool to the touch.

Ice plant foliage grows close to the ground and provides a quick, thick cover. The succulent green leaves may vary in shade, depending on the species or variety. Plants have daisylike flowers in colors ranging from yellow to deep purple to red. Plants may bloom in winter and again in summer, often producing flowers sporadically.

D. nubigenum is a hardy variety with emerald-green foliage that sometimes darkens to reddish purple and yellow flowers. *D. floribundum* 'Starburst' has magenta flowers with bright white centers and yellow stamens. Its foliage is olive-green with a silvery sheen.

Like other ice plants, it loves hot, dry, sunny locations. Ice plant does well in almost any well-drained soil and requires little watering.

CARE INSTRUCTIONS: Ground-cover beds of ice plant may require occasional thinning. Propagate from cuttings or division.

USES: Hot, dry locations.

Known to Californians as the freeway plant, ice plant thrives in hot, dry conditions with little care.

DIANTHUS

Pinks and Sweet William

Pinks make a fine ground cover with many flower color options.

- Hardy in Zones 4 to 10
- Deciduous to evergreen herbaceous perennial
- Up to 2 feet tall
- Space 12 to 15 inches
- Full sun
- Moderate to frequent watering

DESCRIPTION: Pinks (*D.* × *allwoodii*) have slender leaves of blue-green-gray that grow in tufts; evergreen in mild climates. Fragrant flowers rise above the plants about 18 inches. A variety of color options and color patterns range from white to pink to dark red. Sweet William (*D. barbatus*) forms loose mats of deep green foliage. Flowers are grouped in flat clusters atop stiff stalks. Colors range from white to pink to dark red, and some are bicolor. Flowers of cheddar pinks (*D. gratianopolitanus*) come in shades of pink and are highly fragrant; foliage is gray-green.

Dianthus make excellent ground covers. They prefer sunny locations and deep, loamy soil but will tolerate poor soil if well-drained.

CARE INSTRUCTIONS: Shear off flower stems after blooming. Propagate pinks from seed or semi-hardwood cuttings taken in mid-May to mid-July, or by layering. Sweet William is best propagated from seed but can be grown from cuttings and division.

USES: Borders; beds.

DUCHESNEA INDICA

Mock Strawberry

Mock strawberries bear edible but tasteless fruit that attract birds.

- Hardy in Zones 6 to 10
- Semi-evergreen perennial
- 4 to 6 inches tall
- Space 12 to 18 inches
- Sun to partial shade
- Moderate watering

DESCRIPTION: Mock strawberry is a trailing plant with dark green, toothed leaves that look like those of garden strawberries. Yellow flowers with bright green, frilly sepals appear from spring to early summer. They are followed by tasteless, strawberry-like fruit in late summer. Plants are evergreen in mild climates.

Like wild strawberries (*Fragaria*) mock strawberry spreads rapidly by runners and forms a dense mat. Mock strawberry foliage is somewhat lower growing; plants can be invasive.

Grow mock strawberry in well-drained soil and sunny to semi-shaded sites.

CARE INSTRUCTIONS: Trim or mow beds each year in early spring to control growth and improve appearance. Plants spread well from runners.

USES: Borders; foundation plantings.

EPIMEDIUM

Barrenwort

Barrenwort can be slow to spread, but once mature it forms a dense ground cover ideal for shady areas.

- Hardy in Zones 4 to 9 (except desert)
- Semi-evergreen perennial
- 6 to 20 inches tall, depending on species
- Space 10 to 12 inches
- Partial to full shade
- Moderate watering

DESCRIPTION: Red barrenwort leaves are often heart-shaped and tinged with bronze or copper. Some may have more lancelike leaves flecked with pink. Small, cup-shaped flowers appear late spring in colors ranging from white to dark pink to violet to yellow. Blooms resemble a bishop's hat, with the petals arching over a central core, and are sometimes called that. They typically reach 1 foot tall. Longspur epimedium (*E. grandiflorum*) is one of the larger species. 'Rose Queen' has large rosy-red blooms and reddish-tinged foliage. Young's barrenwort (*E.* × *youngianum*) is the shortest at 6 to 8 inches. 'Niveum' blooms in white, 'Roseum' in rose.

Plants need moist, humus-rich soil and partial shade. They are slow to fill a space, but form a dense ground cover at maturity.

CARE INSTRUCTIONS: Protect from severe winds and late frosts. Cut back old foliage in winter. Propagate by seed or division in spring or fall.

USES: Borders; shady areas.

ERIGERON KARVINSKIANUS

Fleabane

- Hardy in Zones 9 and 10 (West), 9 (East)
- Evergreen perennial
- 20 inches tall
- Space 12 inches
- Sun to partial shade
- Low to moderate watering

DESCRIPTION: Fleabane offers finely textured leaves in an array of green hues. Daisylike flowers ranging in color from white to pink to violet with yellow centers cover plants during summer.

Plants do best in moderately fertile, well-drained soil and full sun but will grow in heavy or light soil. They compete well with roots of other trees and shrubs.

CARE INSTRUCTIONS: Keep plants moist during growing season. Provide winter protection. Shear after flowering is complete. Propagate by division in spring or early fall, by basal or softwood cuttings in early summer, or by sowing seed in autumn or spring.

USES: Borders; interplanted with bulbs and other flowers.

Bright, daisylike blooms make fleabane a favorite ground cover to mix with bulbs and other flowers.

ERODIUM

Crane's Bill

- Hardiness varies
- Evergreen perennial
- 2 to 3 inches tall
- Space 6 to 12 inches
- Full sun to light shade
- Moderate to frequent watering

DESCRIPTION: Also known as stork's bills or heron's bills; these plants form 6- to 9-inch-wide mounds of blue-green scalloped leaves. Clusters of tiny geranium-like flowers, often speckled or veined in white to pink to purple, appear in late spring to early summer. Corsican crane's bill (*E. corsicum*) has pink flowers marked with bright pink veins (Zone 4, except in desert regions). Rock or alpine geranium (*E. reichardii*) has white- and pink-flowering cultivars (Zone 7). 'Plenum' is a cultivar with double pink blooms. *E. chrysanthum* has silvery leaves and yellow flowers (Zone 7).

All thrive in moist, well-drained soil and full sun.

CARE INSTRUCTIONS: Protect roots in winter in colder climates. Propagate from seed sown in fall or spring, by division in spring, or from semi-hardwood cuttings taken in summer.

USES: Borders; rock gardens.

Crane's bill works well in border plantings and rock gardens where it receives full sun.

EUONYMUS FORTUNEI

Wintercreeper

- Hardy in Zones 5 to 9
- Woody evergreen to deciduous shrub or vine
- 4 to 24 inches tall
- Space 2 feet
- Sun to partial shade
- Moderate to frequent watering

DESCRIPTION: One of the most common ground covers on the market, *Euonymus* comes in many forms. 'Coloratus' grows to 2 feet tall; its leaves turn purple during winter. Other cultivars: 'Emerald 'n' Gold' (leaves edged in yellow); 'Longwood' (4 inches tall); 'Argenteo-variegatus' has green leaves edged in silvery white; 'Emerald Gaiety' is similar and may be easier to find.

Wintercreeper grows in almost any soil. It tolerates alkaline soil and shade. Some plants climb trees and buildings. For the best fall color, grow deciduous species in sun.

CARE INSTRUCTIONS: Regularly pinch plants to keep them from becoming leggy. Propagate by seed in fall; cuttings and suckers in fall, sometimes spring; layering starting in September. Problems: spider mites; thrips; scale insects (dry soil promotes them).

USES: Slopes and banks; under conifers, evergreens, and low-growing hedges; foundation plantings.

'Emerald Gaiety' wintercreeper adds year-round color and diversity to the landscape.

Ferns

Ferns flourish in humid climates and humus-rich soils. They range in height from 1 to 2 feet. Many spread by rhizomes and form large areas of ground cover. They're perfect for shady spots under trees.

■ **MAIDENHAIR FERN:**
Maidenhair fern (*Adiantum pedatum*), a deciduous to semi-evergreen perennial, produces

Ferns are ideal ground covers in shady areas with moist soil.

Maidenhair fern's feathery, delicate foliage adds grace to a woodland setting.

graceful, delicate fronds on wiry stems that can grow 18 to 24 inches long. It ranges from 6 to 24 inches tall and spreads to a width of 3 to 5 feet. Plants are hardy in Zones 3 to 8. Southern maidenhair fern (*A. capillus-veneris*) is similar to *A. pedatum* but reaches only 18 inches tall and is hardy only to Zone 10.

Maidenhair ferns prefer lime-rich, moist soil to keep their delicate roots from drying out.

Plant 8 to 14 inches apart in partial sun to full shade. These ferns spread by rhizomes and need moderate to frequent watering. Topdress with fresh compost in March and apply a weak liquid fertilizer occasionally. If they become overcrowded, divide in spring as soon as the fronds begin to unfurl. Propagate by division or by sowing spores.

■ **LADY FERN AND JAPANESE PAINTED FERN:** *Athyrium* includes a large group of hardy, deciduous perennial ferns native to temperate and tropical regions (Zones 4 to 11). The lady fern (*A. filix-femina*)

has rich green fronds that grow from 1 to 2 feet in length. The Japanese painted fern (*A. nipponicum* 'Pictum') has grayish green leaves tinted with purple, with dark purple stalks and midribs. Plants are 1 to 2 feet tall.

These ferns need moist, neutral to acid soil and can be grown almost anywhere in the United States. Fronds will turn brown after a hard frost.

Space plants 2 feet apart in light to moderate shade. Give them moderate to frequent watering and protect them from wind. Propagate by division in spring or by sowing spores in summer.

■ **WOOD FERNS:** Wood ferns (*Dryopteris* spp.) are easy to cultivate and ideal for planting in open woodlands or in shady spots in

Wood ferns can be deciduous or evergreen and can be grown in full sun if well-watered.

Zones 3 to 7. This group includes ferns that can be deciduous to evergreen; they form clumps of finely divided foliage. Some have fronds tipped in yellow or brown, or are pinkish or yellowish when young and turn green as they mature. They grow up to 2 feet tall.

These ferns need fertile soil rich in organic matter. They tolerate full sun if they get plenty of water, but they do best in shady, moist places.

Space plants 2 feet apart in partial sun to shade; water frequently. Propagate by division in February and March, or by spores.

■ **SHIELD FERNS:** *Polystichum* includes evergreen and deciduous, and tender and hardy species. They are found in many parts of the world. Their fronds vary in length from 2 to 4 feet. Christmas fern (*P. acrostichoides*) has evergreen fronds 1½ to 2 feet tall, and the plant has a semi-upright—or shuttlecock—habit. It is hardy in Zones 4 to 8. Soft-shield fern (*P. setiferum*) is also evergreen. Its fronds are more finely divided than those of Christmas fern and can grow to 4 feet long. Look for shorter cultivars such as 'Divisilobum', which grows 20 inches tall. 'Proliferum' is a dainty plant, 12 to 18 inches tall. It is hardy in Zones 5 to 7.

Shield ferns prefer moist, friable (or crumbly), well-drained soil. Space them 2 feet apart. Divide in early spring and plant 3 feet apart in partial to deep shade. Protect plants from sun and drying winds, and give them moderate to frequent water. Propagate by division in spring or sowing spores in summer.

■ **JAPANESE HOLLY FERN:**
Japanese holly fern (*Cyrtomium falcatum*) makes a handsome, dense ground cover in mild climates. Fronds are shiny, leathery, and light yellowish green, and grow to about 2½ feet long. Plants tolerate drier air and more sun than many ferns but prefer a rich, moist soil. Space them 18 inches apart. Do not plant them too deep or crowns may rot. Hose off dusty leaves and watch for brown scale. Holly ferns are hardy to Zone 9.

FICUS PUMILA

Creeping Fig

- Hardy in Zones 9 and 10
- Evergreen vine
- To 2 feet tall if trained to trail
- Space 12 to 18 inches
- Partial shade
- Moderate watering

DESCRIPTION: Soft, green creeping fig leaves are heart-shaped and tender when young, but they become leathery and more oval-shaped as they mature. Variegated varieties, which have white edges, are available.

Creeping fig clings to rocks, bricks, and wood to form a fine-textured, light green carpet. Plants also grow up walls. Creeping fig needs moist but well-drained soil; it does not tolerate dry soil. Plants grow best in partial shade.
CARE INSTRUCTIONS: Prune as needed to control growth. Direct sun or frost can scorch leaves. Problem: spider mites.
USES: Covering walls and rocks.

Creeping fig clings to rocks and walls as well as soil, forming a lush carpet over drab, hard surfaces.

FRAGARIA

Wild Strawberry

- Hardy in Zones 6 to 10
- Semi-evergreen perennial
- 6 to 12 inches tall
- Space 12 to 18 inches
- Sun to partial shade
- Moderate to frequent watering

DESCRIPTION: An ancestor of all commercial strawberries, wild strawberry (*F. chiloensis*) forms a thick, dark green mat. Plants have white, strawberry-like blooms in spring followed by small, edible but not too tasty, red fruit. 'Pink Panda'

is the most ornamental, with pink flowers from spring through frost but fewer fruit. Most plants spread by runners, but the Alpine strawberry (*F. vesca* 'Semperflorens') is more of a clump-former.

All do best in full sun and deep, fertile, moisture-retentive but well-drained slightly acid soil, such as loam or sandy loam. They do not tolerate very acid or alkaline soils.
CARE INSTRUCTIONS: In cold regions, cover plants with winter mulch. Mow annually in early spring to keep appearance neat and promote regrowth. Propagate by division or installing new plants. Problems: verticillium wilt; nematodes; spider mites.

USES: Underplanting for widely spaced shrubs or other flowers.

'Pink Panda' is a wild strawberry variety with pink, rather than white, flowers.

GALAX URCEOLATA

Wandflower

- Hardy in Zones 5 to 8 (except desert)
- Evergreen perennial
- 6 to 24 inches tall
- Space 12 inches
- Shade
- Moderate to frequent watering

DESCRIPTION: Wandflower has large, leathery, heart-shaped leaves. The effect is similar to European wild ginger, but wandflower tends to grow into clumps of whorled leaves. Foliage is glossy green in summer

and turns bronze in fall and winter if plants receive sufficient sunlight. Small white flowers that rise above the foliage on spikes appear in late spring and early summer. Foliage will grow to 6 to 9 inches; flower spikes may grow as tall as 2 feet or more in summer.

Wandflower needs full shade and moist, organic, acid soil.
CARE INSTRUCTIONS: Propagate by division in spring or fall.
USES: Shady spots; under shrubs and trees.

Wandflower blooms appear in late spring. Foliage turns from green to bronze in fall and winter.

GALIUM ODORATUM

Sweet Woodruff

Crushed sweet woodruff smells like freshly mown hay. It is ideal for shady areas under trees and shrubs.

- Hardy in Zones 5 to 10 (except desert)
- Perennial
- 6 to 12 inches tall
- Space 12 inches
- Partial to full shade
- Moderate to frequent watering

DESCRIPTION: When sweet woodruff leaves are crushed, they emit a fragrance similar to freshly mown hay. The narrow, rough-edged leaves are arranged in whorls along the stem. Leaf color changes from bright green in summer to light brown in winter. Tiny star-shaped white or yellow flowers appear in clusters. Plants spread by underground runners, and once established, plants spread quickly.

Sweet woodruff grows best in any good-quality, slightly acid soil in part sun or shade. In northern climates where summers are cool, sweet woodruff tolerates sun. Plants can be invasive.

CARE INSTRUCTIONS: Pull runners that creep outside boundaries of beds. Propagate by seed or division.

USES: Underplanting for thick shrubs; any shaded spot; interspersed with lilies; leaves and stems are used to make May wine and potpourris.

GAULTHERIA

Wintergreen

The foliage of wintergreen, also known as teaberry or checkerberry, changes to purple in late fall.

- Hardy in Zones 4 to 10
- Evergreen shrub
- 3 to 10 inches tall
- Space 12 to 18 inches
- Partial to full shade
- Frequent watering

DESCRIPTION: Wintergreen (G. procumbens), also called teaberry or checkerberry, is a beautiful, herblike, woody evergreen ground cover. Its round leaves become leathery with age and turn a rich burgundy in spring and fall. Crushing them releases aromatic wintergreen oil.

Small, nodding, white bell-shaped flowers are followed by edible red berries that turn pink with age; the berries attract birds and other wildlife.

Creeping pearlberry (G. hispidula) is a dwarf species that grows 2 to 3 inches tall. Its tiny white flowers in late spring are followed by white berries in fall.

Choose a shady location for these shrubs in moist but well-drained, acid soil.

CARE INSTRUCTIONS: Propagate from seed sown in spring, from stem cuttings taken in summer, or by division.

USES: Bogs; woodlands.

GAYLUSSACIA BRACHYCERA

Box Huckleberry

Box huckleberry leaves change from green to red in fall and winter. Plants bear black, edible fruit.

- Hardy in Zones 6 to 8
- Woody evergreen to deciduous shrub
- Up to 2 feet tall
- Space 3 to 4 feet
- Sun to partial shade
- Moderate watering

DESCRIPTION: Box huckleberry is a low-growing evergreen shrub with lustrous dark green leaves. Foliage turns bronze, to red, to reddish purple in fall and winter. Small, urn-shaped, red flowers appear in clusters during late spring and are followed by round, black, edible fruit, which resemble blueberries, in late summer.

Plants grow best in moist, acid—pH of 4.5 to 5.5—soil and partial shade, the same conditions preferred by other members of the heather family. Box huckleberry makes an excellent companion plant to heather, and it is an ideal choice for use under pine trees. In full sun, the tips of its branches and leaves become reddish.

CARE INSTRUCTIONS: Propagate box huckleberry by cuttings in spring or seed in fall. Problems: leaf gall; powdery mildew; rust.

USES: Under trees and shrubs; as edging.

GAZANIA RIGENS

Gazania

- Hardy in Zones 9 and 10 (West)
- Evergreen perennial
- Up to 12 inches tall
- Space 12 to 19 inches
- Sun
- Low to moderate watering

DESCRIPTION: This extremely frost-tender plant forms rosettes of tough, spoon-shaped leaves that are waxy green above and silvery white below. Large, showy, daisylike flowers of yellow, orange, pink, mahogany, white, or bicolor appear from late spring through summer and intermittently the rest of the year. Flowers close at night or in cloudy weather.

Gazania grows well in full sun and moist, well-drained soil in temperate regions.

CARE INSTRUCTIONS: Water at least every other week in hot weather. In colder climates, cover with mulch in winter. Propagate by seed or cuttings taken in August or division in fall or spring.

USES: Desert settings; filler amid new shrubs; banks and slopes; median or parking strips.

Gazania is a bright addition to a desert landscape.

GELSEMIUM SEMPERVIRENS

Carolina Jessamine

- Hardy in Zones 8 to 10
- Evergreen woody vine
- Up to 2 feet tall if allowed to trail
- Space 3 feet
- Sun to partial shade
- Moderate watering

DESCRIPTION: This versatile vine has fine-textured, slender leaves that are shiny, dark green in summer and may turn purplish in winter. In particularly cold winters, plants will lose their leaves. Fragrant yellow flower clusters appear in late winter to early spring and bloom sporadically through the spring.

Plants do fine in average soil and tolerate hot sun. Although plants grow in partial shade, they bloom better in full sun.

CARE INSTRUCTIONS: Prune after flowering to encourage branching and control growth.

USES: Slopes and walls; climbing posts, mailboxes, and trellises; hot settings.

NOTE: Plants are toxic when ingested. Do not allow children to sip the nectar.

Carolina jessamine is a vine that does especially well in hot climates.

GENISTA

Broom

- Hardy in Zones 6 to 9
- Woody semi-evergreen to deciduous shrub
- Up to 2 feet tall
- Space 2 feet
- Low to moderate watering

DESCRIPTION: Also known as woadwaxen, broom can be evergreen or deciduous, depending on the species. The common name arises from the whiplike branches. All species have sparsely covered branches and masses of yellow to golden pealike flowers from late spring to late summer. Lydia broom (*G. lydia*) is a dwarf deciduous species with slender, drooping branches. Silky-leaf broom (*G. pilosa*) is deciduous and grows to 18 inches; its has silky hairs on its flowers and foliage. Dyer's greenwood (*G. tinctoria*) grows up to 2 feet tall and is hardy to Zone 4.

Brooms live in a variety of soil types, preferring dry, well-drained, poor-quality, slightly acid to alkaline soil. They endure heat well.

CARE INSTRUCTIONS: Brooms do not transplant well. Shelter them from wind. Pinch shoots annually to encourage bushiness. Propagate from seed sown in early spring.

USES: Hot, dry settings (except desert) and coastal areas; drought-prone slopes or banks.

Lydia broom does well in coastal areas and on drought-prone slopes or banks.

GERANIUM

Cranesbill

'Anne Folkard' cranesbill grows 2 feet tall and 3 feet wide, and blooms from midsummer to fall.

■ Hardy in Zones 5 to 10
■ Evergreen or deciduous perennial
■ 2 feet tall
■ Space 1 to 2 feet
■ Sun
■ Moderate to frequent watering

DESCRIPTION: Although similar in genus name, cranesbills are not directly related to the common potted geranium. Cranesbills grow from 1 to 2 feet tall and have lobed leaves ranging in color from light to dark green. The leaves of some species turn red in fall; some have furry or wrinkled leaves. Their large, cup-shaped flowers range in color from white to hot pink to violet blue, sometimes marked with dark veins of maroon to purple. 'Ballerina' gray leaf cranesbill (*G. cinereum*) grows 6 inches tall and has pink flowers in late spring. 'Johnson Blue' has clear blue flowers and grows to 18 inches tall. A few species grow 4 feet tall, so read labels carefully.

These plants grow well in ordinary, fertile garden soil that has excellent drainage, in sun or light shade.

CARE INSTRUCTIONS: Cut back trailing stems before winter. Propagate by division or seed in spring or fall, or cuttings taken in summer.

USES: Borders; trailing over walls.

Ornamental Grasses

■ BLUE FESCUE

Festuca glauca is one of the finest ornamental grass ground covers. It forms 2- to 10-inch-tall tufts of slender blue foliage, which may turn green in winter. Flowers are straw-colored and can detract from the plant's overall effect.

Plants need well-drained soil and tolerate dry conditions; they don't do well in wet areas. Mow to 2 inches annually. Divide every two to three years. Space plants 6 to 12 inches apart in a sunny location; use the closer spacing for fast coverage. Water moderately. Propagate by division. Evergreen; hardy in Zones 3 to 10.

■ BLUE OAT GRASS

Helictotrichon sempervirens, a herbaceous perennial grass, forms lovely tufted clumps of foliage with arching bluish leaves similar to blue fescue, only larger. It grows to 2 feet tall. It flowers occasionally but may not flower in cold climates.

Plants prefer full to partial sun and well-drained soil. They develop best in dry soil. Water lightly. Mow or cut back once a year. Space plants 6 to 8 inches apart. Propagate by division in spring. Hardy in Zones 4 to 10.

■ VELVET GRASS

Holcus lanatus and *H. mollis* have long, linear leaves and grow in clumps. Leaves may be hairy or fuzzy and can be solid green or variegated with white stripes. Spikes of tiny purplish white flowers form in summer. Plants grow 12 to 18 inches tall and can spread widely.

Velvet grass prefers average soil that is moist but well-drained and sunny to partially shaded locations. Space plants 6 to 12 inches apart and water moderately. Propagate by division in spring. Evergreen; hardy in Zones 5 to 10.

■ JAPANESE BLOOD GRASS

Imperata cylindrica 'Red Baron' grows 12 to 18 inches tall with slender red leaves that deepen in color in fall. Green species are invasive and listed on the federal register of noxious weeds; it is illegal to grow or sell them.

Plants prefer full or partial sun and fertile, moist, but well-drained soil. Shear or mow annually. Space plants 6 to 12 inches apart and water moderately. If all-green shoots appear, remove and destroy plant immediately. Propagate by division. Semi-evergreen; may be evergreen in mild climates. Hardy in Zones 5 to 10.

■ RIBBON GRASS

Phalaris arundinacea 'Picta' is a lovely but invasive grass. Its leaves are green striped with white. Flowers rarely appear and are not showy. Plants grow up to 3 feet tall.

Plants prefer damp, shady borders by water but tolerate a wide range of soil types and moisture levels. Mow or shear in late summer to 6 inches to bring on fresh growth. Space 12 inches apart in sun to partial shade. Propagate by seed or division. Perennial; hardy in Zones 4 to 10.

Ribbon grass, which spreads rapidly, requires little care.

'Elijah Blue' fescue adds unusual color and diversity to the landscape.

GYPSOPHILA REPENS

Creeping Baby's Breath

- Hardy in Zones 3 to 10
- Deciduous herbaceous perennial
- 4 to 8 inches tall
- Space 12 inches
- Sun
- Moderate watering

DESCRIPTION: Creeping baby's breath, which is native to Europe, is a delicate-looking plant with lance-shaped, blue-green leaves and tiny, double white to pink flowers in summer. Some baby's breath species can reach 2 feet tall, so read plant labels carefully before buying. 'Rosea' and 'Pink Baby' have pink flowers, as does 'Dorothy Teacher'. 'Alba' has white blooms. A few cultivars of common baby's breath (*G. paniculata*) are low enough to grow as ground covers. 'Viette's Dwarf' grows 12 to 18 inches and has double pink flowers. 'Pink Fairy' is 18 inches tall with double flowers.

Baby's breath prefers deep, moderately fertile soil that is well-drained but moist. It does not transplant well once established and needs plenty of space to grow.
CARE INSTRUCTIONS: Prune or shear after first flowering to encourage second flowering. Mulch in winter in colder climates. Propagate from seed sown in fall.
USES: Interspersed with roses, cranesbills, and other perennials.

Creeping baby's breath is a delicate plant that works well planted with other flowers.

Heaths and Heathers

■ **SCOTCH HEATHER** (*Calluna vulgaris*), a woody evergreen shrub, is a true heather. It is 6 to 24 inches tall (depending on species) and spreads 2 to 8 feet with dark green, sometimes gold to brown, foliage on dense branches. It has a mounding, spreading growth habit. Small, bell-shaped flowers in pink, purple, or white on spikes appear in mid- to late summer and, in some varieties, to fall. Flowers attract bees. Cultivars with different growth habits and flowers are available.

Grow Scotch heather in acid, well-drained soil in sun or light shade. Plants do best in cool, moist climates. They will grow in poor, well-drained, acid soil.

Before new growth begins in spring, prune previous year's growth at its base. In cold climates, mulch plants with evergreen branches in winter. Space plants 12 to 18 inches apart. Apply acid fertilizer in late winter, again in early spring. Do not add lime. In hot, dry climates, water frequently to keep soil moist. Propagate from seed, cuttings in July or August, or layering in spring. Problems: Japanese beetles. Hardy in Zones 5 to 9 (except desert).

■ **IRISH HEATH** (*Daboecia cantabrica*) is a 2-foot-tall evergreen perennial shrub with thin stems and small, oval leaves that are dark green on top, white underneath. Spikes of bell-shaped flowers in white, purple, mauve, and red in early summer to late fall. Some have bicolored or double-petaled flowers. Bicolored plants usually have white and rosy-purple-striped flowers on the same bush, often in the same cluster.

Plants like moist, well-drained, organic soil and a sunny location. They do fine in partial shade, but sprawl and may need more frequent pruning. Space plants 2 feet apart and protect from cold winds. They need low to moderate watering. Propagate from seed in spring or fall, or from cuttings taken in July or August. Hardy in Zones 6 to 10.

■ **TRUE HEATHS** (*Erica carnea*) range from dwarf shrubs to small trees; 12 to 18 inches tall is most common. The evergreen foliage ranges from gold and silver to lime green. Scented, bell-shaped flowers range in color from white to lavender to scarlet.

Plants prefer full to part sun and acid, organic soil that holds moisture but also is well-drained. They will tolerate neutral soil. Prune after flowering to promote bushiness. Add peat moss to soil before planting to enhance growth. Plants generally do not need fertilizer. Protect them from cold, drying winds. Space plants 18 inches apart; water frequently. Propagate by sowing seed in spring or from cuttings taken in June for tender species and September to November for hardier heaths. They perform best in cool, moist climates in Zones 6 to 8.

Heathers bloom in a variety of pinks, purples, and whites.

Golden foliage is common in heathers and true heaths. Plants help stabilize slopes.

HEBE

Shrubby Veronica

Shrubby veronica is an evergreen shrub that grows well in coastal areas and rock gardens.

- Hardy in Zones 8 to 10 (West, except desert)
- Woody evergreen shrub
- 8 to 18 inches
- Space 3 to 4 feet
- Sun to light shade
- Moderate to frequent watering

DESCRIPTION: These evergreen shrubs come in a variety of sizes, from small, low-growing species to large shrubs, so take care to buy a ground cover species. They have small leaves that often are glossy and may be light to dark green to blue-green in color. Most produce panicles of four-lobed white or pale lilac flowers in late spring and summer; some bloom through fall. Among the ground cover plants are *H. canterburiensis* 'Prostrata', 18 inches tall with white flowers and tiny leaves in midsummer and *H. decumbens*, 14 inches tall by 5 feet wide, with red margins on its leaves and white flowers in spring. 'Carl Teschner' (also called 'Youngii') is 8 inches tall and 2 feet wide with lilac flowers.

Shrubby veronicas are well-adapted to coastal climates. They need full sun and well-drained soil to thrive.

CARE INSTRUCTIONS: Prune in spring to restrict growth and improve appearance. Propagate from cuttings in summer.

USES: Coastal areas; rock gardens.

HEDERA

Algerian Ivy and English Ivy

- Hardiness varies
- Evergreen to deciduous woody vine
- 2 feet as a ground cover
- Space 12 to 18 inches
- Shade to sun
- Moderate to frequent watering

English ivy is an all-purpose ground cover for sun or shade.

DESCRIPTION: Many types of climbing or trailing ivies are available as ground covers. Most have shiny, leathery leaves in a wide range of shapes and sizes.

■ **ENGLISH IVY** (*H. helix*) is among the most commonly used ivies. Many cultivars are available offering different leaf shapes, sizes, and colorings. Most have lobed leaves in various shades of green. Some have variegated leaves or leaves with splotches of gray and white that may turn pink in winter.

'Anna Marie' has gray-green leaves with cream variegation. 'Buttercup' displays leaves that are pale green in shade, yellow in sun, and maroon in cold weather. Leaves of 'Fluffy Ruffles' are frilled; those of 'Glacier' are variegated with white edges. 'Maple Leaf' has deeply divided leaves with pointed lobes.

Among the most hardy cultivars—to Zone 4—are 'Baltica' (smaller leaves), 'Bulgaria', 'Rumania', Thorndale' (heart-shaped leaves with white veins), 'Wilsonii', and 'Ogalalla'.

English ivies root at every node on a stem and can be invasive.

■ **ALGERIAN IVY** (*H. algeriensis*) is a tough plant that does well in mild-winter regions. It has large, triangular, lobed leaves that are typically leathery and may be deep green or variegated. It produces inconspicuous flowers and berries, and spreads rapidly. The plants need protection from full sun in desert regions. Hardy to Zone 8. 'Gloire de Marengo' has wide leaves with white to cream edges and gray-green variegation.

Algerian ivies grow well in average soil and full sun to partial shade. Those grown in full sun may require more water than those grown in shade.

CARE INSTRUCTIONS: Plant ivy in well-drained, rich, fairly moist soil. They grow best in shade, but once established will tolerate full sun if kept watered. Algerian ivy is better for sunny situations.

English ivy is more drought-tolerant than Algerian ivy, but in hot, dry regions, all ivies require regular watering. Take care to not overwater in shady areas where the soil is slow to dry.

Mow ivy beds yearly to every other year just before new growth begins. Mow Algerian ivy in July in areas with long growing seasons. Propagate from seed or softwood to semi-hardwood cuttings. Problems: leaf spots, snails, slugs, may provide a habitat for small rodents.

USES: Under trees and shrubs.

HELIANTHEMUM NUMMULARIUM

Sun Rose

- Hardy in Zones 6 to 10
- Evergreen to semi-evergreen shrubby perennial
- 8 inches tall
- Space 24 to 30 inches
- Sun
- Low to moderate watering

DESCRIPTION: Hairy, gray-green foliage forms mounds of sprawling stems. Small, roselike flowers in bright colors appear in summer and continue through fall. Individual flowers last only a day, but the plants bloom over a long period. Colors include red, peach, copper, pink, yellow, and white. Each plant forms a clump about 3 feet wide. Branches root as they spread, eventually creating a thick mat.

Plants need well-drained, infertile, neutral to alkaline soil, and tolerate hot, dry conditions well. They do best in dry soil and will not tolerate high humidity.
CARE INSTRUCTIONS: Shear after summer blooming and again in spring. Protect with mulch or cover with evergreen branches in colder climates.
USES: Rock gardens; walls; slopes; hot, dry settings; firebreaks.

Sun rose, with its hairy foliage and bright flowers, looks lovely tumbling over walls and down slopes.

HELLEBORUS

Christmas Rose and Lenten Rose

- Hardy in Zones 4 to 10
- Evergreen or deciduous perennial
- 12 to 18 inches tall
- Space 12 to 18 inches
- Partial shade to sun
- Moderate watering

DESCRIPTION: An early delight for winter-weary gardeners, lenten and Christmas roses are some of the finest low-growing plants in cultivation. They have bright to dark green leathery leaves and clusters of large, nodding, cup-shaped flowers that are white, cream, pink, violet-purple, maroon, or greenish yellow, sometimes with green centers or flecked with purple-red specks. Christmas rose (*H. niger*) blooms in late winter in mild climates. Lenten rose (*H. orientalis*) is an early spring bloomer.

Both plants prefer fertile, moist soil that is well-drained and alkaline, in sun or partial shade.
CARE INSTRUCTIONS: Protect from cold winds. In spring, water with liquid fertilizer. Propagate by division in fall or by sowing seed.
USES: Underplantings; foundation plantings.

Hellebores add color and beauty to any landscape and are especially ideal as foundation plantings.

HEMEROCALLIS HYBRIDS

Daylily

- Hardy in Zones 3 to 10
- Evergreen to deciduous perennial
- Up to 2 feet tall
- Space 12 to 18 inches
- Sun to partial shade
- Moderate to frequent watering

DESCRIPTION: Daylilies are in the lily family but are not true lilies. Their flowers last only a day, but are borne in succession over two to six weeks in summer. Some species are evergreen and range in height from 12 to 15 inches up to 5 feet; buy a variety with an appropriate height for ground cover use, such as yellow 'Stella de Oro', reblooming, 12 inches tall; 'Black Eyed Stella', yellow with crimson, 14 to 22 inches tall, long bloom period; and lemon-yellow 'Irish Limerick', 12 to 15 inches tall, reportedly good as a firebreak. Daylilies bloom in a wide range of colors, from creamy white through yellow, brilliant orange, and red, pink, and purple. Flowers may be one color, banded, streaked, or spotted. Some are fragrant; some have ruffled edges or double blooms.

Plants thrive in nearly all soil types but prefer fertile, humus-rich, and moist, but well-drained, soil. Flowers are best in sunny locations.
CARE INSTRUCTIONS: Propagate by seed or division in spring or fall. Problems: slugs, snails, midges.
USES: Borders; ditches; gullies.

Daylilies, with their stout roots, form a thick mat perfect for holding the soil on sunny slopes and banks.

HEUCHERA

Coral Bells and Alumroot

Coral bells are shade-loving plants with flowers that range from white to scarlet.

- Hardy in Zones 4 to 10
- Deciduous to evergreen perennial
- 12 to 18 inches tall
- Space 6 to 12 inches
- Sun to partial shade
- Moderate watering

DESCRIPTION: Coral bells (*H. sanguinea*) grow into mounds treasured for beautiful foliage and delicate flowers. They form clumps with light green, ivy-shaped leaves and, in summer, tiny bell-shaped flowers on long, slender stems. Flower colors range from white to scarlet.

Alumroot (both *H. micrantha* and *H. americana*) is quickly surpassing coral bells in popularity. Breeding has led to numerous, maybe even hundreds, of new cultivars, such as 'Palace Purple', 'Amethyst Myst', 'Oakington Jewel', 'Chocolate Ruffles', 'Pewter Moon', and 'Velvet Night'. You can now find plants with foliage from bronze to dark maroon to silver, with white to light pink to hot pink flowers.

Plants prefer light, loamy soil that is moist but well-drained, and sunny or partially shaded sites. Shade is best for plants in the South.

CARE INSTRUCTIONS: Deadhead spent flowers. Propagate by division in spring or fall using only younger outside portions of the crown.

USES: Shady areas.

HOSTA

Hostas

Hostas are a perennial favorite for use in shady spots because of their lovely and diverse foliage.

- Hardy in Zones 3 to 9 (except some desert regions)
- Deciduous perennial
- 6 to 36 inches tall
- Space 12 to 36 inches, depending on type
- Partial to full shade
- Frequent watering

DESCRIPTION: Hostas are cherished for their striking foliage and elegant flowers. Leaves come in a wide variety of textures and colors, including green; green variegated with white, cream, or yellow; blue-green; golden yellow; and greenish yellow. Leaves may be long and straplike or broadly oval or heart-shaped. Edges may be ruffled, and leaf tips may be curled or twisted. Many species have spikes of tubular, trumpet-, or bell-shaped flowers in shades of purple, pink, or white; some are fragrant.

Hostas prefer moist but well-drained, humus-rich, neutral soil and partial shade. Some, especially blue-leaf varieties, tolerate full shade. In cool climates, hostas, especially yellow-leaved varieties, can take full sun. Plants survive short dry spells but do not do well in arid regions.

CARE INSTRUCTIONS: Mulch in spring to keep soil moist. Propagate by seed or division in early spring. Problems: slugs, snails.

USES: Damp shade.

'Chameleon' houttuynia thrives in boggy, areas, lighting them up with mottled red-and-cream foliage.

HOUTTUYNIA CORDATA 'CHAMELEON'

Houttuynia

- Hardy in Zones 5 to 10 (West, except desert)
- Deciduous perennial
- 6 to 12 inches tall
- Space 12 to 18 inches
- Sun to shade
- Frequent watering

DESCRIPTION: These are wonderful plants, with colorful bluish green, heart-shaped leaves mottled with cream or red splotches that form a dense mat.

In early summer, small cone-shaped flowers surrounded by white petal-like bracts appear, but flowers are not particularly ornamental. It's the foliage that drives the popularity of this plant.

Under ideal conditions—moist sites, especially near natural streams and ponds—houttuynia can be aggressive, spreading widely.

Plants grow well in wet soil, including shallow water.

CARE INSTRUCTIONS: Plants can become invasive. Propagate them from divisions or rooted stem cuttings in spring.

USES: Wet sites, such as bogs, margins of water gardens, ponds, and streams.

HYPERICUM

St. Johnswort

- Hardy in Zones 6 to 10
- Woody deciduous to evergreen shrub
- Up to 24 inches tall
- Space 12 to 18 inches
- Sun to partial shade
- Moderate watering

DESCRIPTION: This genus includes more than 300 perennials, evergreen and deciduous trees, and shrubs with large leaves and bright or golden-yellow flowers in summer and fall. Ground-cover species include Aaron's beard (*H. calycinum*), a dwarf evergreen shrub with large leaves and yellow flowers. It grows well in dry, shady spots but can be invasive. Moser's St. Johnswort (*H. × moserianum*) grows to about 20 inches high with red and gold flowers from midsummer to mid-fall. 'Tricolor' has green-, pink-, and white-variegated leaves, and grows well in sheltered areas. It's hardy only to Zone 7.

St. Johnswort thrives in any type of well-drained soil and in sun or partial shade.

CARE INSTRUCTIONS: St. Johnswort rarely requires pruning; however, Aaron's beard should be cut to the ground every two years in spring. Propagate from cuttings taken in June or July or from seed. Aaron's beard can be propagated by division. Problem: rust.

USES: Fast coverage; dry settings.

St. Johnswort is a fast-growing ground cover with bright flowers. It does well in dry locales.

IBERIS SEMPERVIRENS

Candytuft

- Hardy in Zones 3 to 8
- Herbaceous evergreen perennial
- 6 to 12 inches tall
- Space 6 to 12 inches
- Sun to partial shade
- Moderate watering

DESCRIPTION: Bushy candytuft plants form tufts or spreading mats that may grow as wide as 3 feet. Its dark green leaves are oblong and evergreen. In early spring and sometimes again in fall, large flat-topped clusters of small white flowers blanket the plants. Several cultivars have more compact growth. 'Autumn Snow' reblooms in fall; 'Little Gem' grows 5 to 8 inches tall; 'October Glory' is an 8-inch-tall rebloomer.

Candytuft prefers sunny spots in well-drained fertile soil with neutral to alkaline pH.

CARE INSTRUCTIONS: Water regularly during the growing season; prune or shear hard after plants bloom to keep stems from becoming leggy. Fall bloomers especially benefit from a yearly shearing. Propagate from seed, from cuttings taken in June, or by division in September.

USES: Over walls and slopes.

Candytuft, magnificent tumbling over walls in sunny spots, blooms in spring and sometimes again in fall.

INDIGOFERA

Indigo

- Hardiness varies
- Deciduous woody shrub or perennial
- Up to 2½ feet tall
- Space 3 feet
- Sun
- Moderate watering

DESCRIPTION: Indigos are shrubby with arching stems. They have glossy, oval, dark green leaves and pealike flowers from mid-summer through fall. Chinese indigo (*I. decora*) is an 18-inch-tall shrub with 4- to 5-inch-long, pale pink, spiky blooms in mid- to late summer; it is hardy to Zone 7. 'Alba', with white flowers is probably most common. *I. pseudotinctoria* is more arching and trailing in habit. It is 2½ feet tall and has light red to pink blooms. Kirilow indigo (*I. kirilowii*) reaches 2½ feet tall and has rose-pink flowers in midsummer. It is the hardiest variety, to Zone 5.

Plants require full sun and fertile, well-drained soil.

CARE INSTRUCTIONS: Indigos grow vigorously and can be invasive. Prune deadwood in spring. Propagate by cuttings in summer and seed in fall.

USES: Erosion control.

Indigo is a trailing shrub that is especially good for controlling erosion on sunny slopes.

JASMINUM

Jasmine

Pink blush Jasmine (J. polyanthum) has intensely fragrant pink blossoms from spring through summer.

- Hardiness varies
- Evergreen to deciduous woody shrub
- 2 feet tall with training
- Space 10 feet
- Sun to partial shade
- Moderate to frequent watering

DESCRIPTION: These viny shrubs grow from a central point to form mounds of arching stems, which root wherever they touch the ground. Stems are so green that deciduous plants may appear evergreen. Most species grow much taller than ground-cover size.

Winter jasmine (*J. nudiflorum*) is deciduous. It grows 3 to 4 feet tall and has yellow flowers in February to March (hardy to Zone 6). Poet's jasmine (*J. officinale*) has fragrant white flowers in summer and grows to 15 feet (Zone 7). Dwarf jasmine (*J. parkeri*) is a compact shrub to 12 inches tall and 16 inches wide; slightly fragrant bright yellow flowers bloom in spring (Zone 7).

Jasmine does well in average soil and sunny locations. Plants tolerate some drought.

CARE INSTRUCTIONS: Remove oldest stems each year or prune all stems to 6 inches above ground every five years. Trim shoots as soon as flowers fade; if pruned too severely or at wrong time, plants stop blooming. Propagate from cuttings.

USES: Banks and slopes.

JUNIPERUS

Juniper

'Wiltonii' juniper is just one of the many creeping junipers available for use as a ground cover.

Junipers work well mixed with other plants in the landscape.

- Hardiness varies
- Evergreen conifer
- Up to 2 feet tall
- Space 4 to 6 feet
- Sun to partial shade
- Low to moderate watering

DESCRIPTION: The original low-maintenance plants, *Juniperus* contains 50 species of evergreen shrubs and trees, offering a wide range of design and site options. Some are small enough for rock gardens; others are so large that one can cover an entire slope. Many ground cover species are available, and many of the taller-growing species have ground cover cultivars.

Creeping juniper (*J. horizontalis*) and Japanese garden juniper (*J. procumbens*) make especially good ground covers. Creeping juniper has soft-textured branches with leaves that turn purplish pink over winter. It is hardy in Zones 3 to 9 or 10. Consider the cultivars 'Blue Chip', which has blue foliage, is 12 inches tall, and spreads 8 to 10 feet, and 'Wiltonii', also called 'Blue Rug', which is 4 to 6 inches tall and 6 to 8 feet wide.

Japanese garden juniper has sharp, short-pointed needles. Plants are generally 8 to 12 inches tall and 10 to 15 feet wide. They are hardy in Zones 5 to 9. 'Nana' is a more compact plant, and 'Green Mound' is 8 inches tall and 6 feet wide.

Savin juniper (*J. sabina*) has several good ground-cover cultivars hardy in Zones 3 to 8. These have a spreading habit with branches that arch into soft mounds. Foliage is light to medium green in summer, but it may turn yellowish in winter. 'Arcadia' has sharp grass-green needles. It grows 18 inches tall and spreads 4 feet. 'Buffalo' has bright green, feathery branches. Plants are 12 inches tall and 8 feet wide.

Shore juniper (*J. conferta*) grows 1 to 2 feet tall and spreads 6 to 9 feet. It is hardy in Zones 6 to 9. 'Emerald Sea' has bright green foliage and grows 10 inches high and 8 feet wide.

Juniper wood, foliage, and berries are often fragrant. Plants can be used in a wide range of soil types, even to hold sandy soil against erosion. They prefer well-drained soil and full to partial sun. In shady sites, plants become spindly and their habit opens up.

Although junipers require little maintenance, they are susceptible to a number of pests, including spider mites; bagworms; juniper blight, twig blight, juniper scale, and root rot.

CARE INSTRUCTIONS: Protect young plants from cold until they have formed hard wood. Propagate juniper from seed, hardwood cuttings, or grafts, or by layering.

USES: Rock gardens; foundation plantings; rough slopes and banks; near the seashore.

LAMIUM

Dead Nettle and Yellow Archangel

- Hardy in Zones 5 to 10
- Deciduous to evergreen perennial
- 6 to 24 inches tall
- Space 18 to 24 inches
- Partial to full shade
- Frequent watering

DESCRIPTION: These plants have a 1- to 3-foot spread, rapidly filling in a bed, then setting seed and cropping up in other parts of your yard. Some are weeds; several are fine ground covers. 'White Nancy' (*L. maculatum*) has mats of silvery pale green leaves and small snow-white flowers from late spring to summer. 'Chequers' has green leaves with a central white stripe and mauve-pink flowers. Yellow archangel (*L. galeobdolon*) has silvery variegated foliage and yellow tubular flowers in early summer.

Plants prefer cool, moist, well-drained, average soil high in organic matter. They do not tolerate winter moisture or extremely dry soil and hot weather.

CARE INSTRUCTIONS: Plants are less likely to be invasive in dry soil. Shear or mow in midsummer. Propagate by division or runners in winter, by seed or division in early spring or fall, or by stem cuttings of nonflowering shoots in midsummer.

USES: Fast coverage; shade; binds soil.

'Hermann's Pride' yellow archangel offers texture and color in shade.

LAMPRANTHUS

Ice Plant

- Hardy in Zones 8 to 10
- Perennial succulent or shrub
- 10 to 24 inches tall
- Space 6 to 12 inches
- Sun
- Low to moderate watering

DESCRIPTION: These flowering succulents have daisylike flowers in a variety of colors. Some flower for a short time; others bloom from spring to fall. Trailing ice plant (*L. spectabilis*) has pinkish lilac flowers in spring and summer and grows 10 inches tall. *L. haworthii* is a bushy variety with candelabra-like leaves of blue-green. It grows up to 2 feet tall with unlimited spread and has large bright pink, magenta, or purple flowers through early fall. *L. aurantiacus* is an erect-growing variety that eventually becomes prostrate, with tapering blue-green leaves and brilliant orange flowers. Both bloom from spring through early fall.

Ice plants grow best in well-drained, sandy loam.

CARE INSTRUCTIONS: In summer, water moderately. Plants become woody with age and should be replaced when they start to wane. Propagate from cuttings taken from March to September.

USES: Xeriscape settings; hot, dry settings.

Ice plants are a good choice for xeriscapes—water-saving landscapes—in hot, dry climates.

LANTANA

Lantana

- Hardy in Zones 9 and 10
- Semi-evergreen shrubby vine
- Up to 2 feet tall
- Space 3 feet
- Sun
- Low to moderate watering

DESCRIPTION: From late spring to fall, lantanas bear rounded clusters of flowers in cream, white, yellow, gold, pink, lavender, orange, and red. Some types combine colors in the same flower cluster. Trailing lantana (*L. montevidensis*) has sprawling stems and lavender blooms; it is more cold-hardy than other lantanas. Shrub lantana (*L. camara*) offers the most diversity with numerous cultivars, such as 'Miss Huff', orange and pink flowers; 'Rainbow', with blooms that change from chiffon yellow to orange to fuchsia-pink; 'Radiation', rich orange-red blooms; 'Weeping Lavender'; and 'Dallas Red'.

Lantanas do well in almost all soil and tolerate dry conditions and heat as well as salt.

CARE INSTRUCTIONS: Do not overwater. Prune deadwood in spring and trim plants to control shape and growth. Propagate by seed in spring or cuttings in summer. Problems: spider mites; aphids; whiteflies.

USES: Seaside settings; deserts.

Trailing lantana blooms from late spring to fall, offering clusters of solid or variegated flowers.

Blue star creeper will grow between pavers, rocks, or stepping-stones.

LAURENTIA FLUVIATILIS

Blue Star Creeper

- Hardy in Zones 8 to 10 (West, except desert)
- Evergreen perennial
- 2 to 5 inches tall
- Space 6 to 12 inches
- Sun to partial shade
- Frequent watering

DESCRIPTION: Blue star creeper has tiny bright green leaves that hug the ground and give a mosslike effect. It has star-shaped flowers of light blue that grow scattered across the surface of the foliage in late spring and summer. As the plant blankets the soil, it seems to flow around rocks and pavers.

Plants do fine in most average soils. They can be grown in areas with hot summers if planted in shade.

CARE INSTRUCTIONS: Water regularly to frequently in summer and fertilize monthly from spring to fall.

USES: Between pavers or stepping-stones; among rocks.

NOTE: Taxonomists have recently changed the name of this genus. You may now find it listed as *Solenopsis*.

LEIOPHYLLUM BUXIFOLIUM

Sand Myrtle

Sand myrtle is an evergreen shrub that works well in rock gardens located in partial shade.

- Hardy in Zones 6 to 10
- Evergreen shrub
- Up to 2 feet tall
- Space 1 to 2 feet
- Partial shade
- Moderate watering

DESCRIPTION: Sand myrtle is an attractive shrub with a rounded habit and tiny, oval, dark green leaves that turn bronze in fall. In spring, large clusters of tiny, white, star-shaped flowers open from pink buds. They have the appearance of bridal-wreath spirea.

The species grows 1 to 2 feet tall by 4 to 5 feet wide. 'Nanum' has pink flowers and is only 2 to 4 inches tall and 12 inches wide. Allegheny sand myrtle (*L. buxifolium prostratum*) is 4 to 10 inches tall by 18 inches wide.

Plants need moist, well-drained, acid soil, well-amended with organic matter. Plants are slow to establish and grow slowly. Sand myrtle withstands coastal conditions but does not tolerate drought.

CARE INSTRUCTIONS: Water as needed and topdress with a peat soil mix. Prune after flowering. Propagate by seed in spring or cuttings in summer.

USES: Rock gardens; edging; seashore plantings.

New Zealand brass buttons favor areas with moist soil and sun to light shade.

LEPTINELLA SQUALIDA

New Zealand Brass Buttons

- Hardy in Zones 8 to 10
- Evergreen to deciduous perennial
- 1 to 6 inches tall
- Space 6 inches
- Sun to light shade
- Moderate to frequent watering

DESCRIPTION: New Zealand brass buttons displays finely cut, gray-green foliage and buttonlike yellow flowers in late spring to early summer. Plants are deciduous in colder climates and evergreen in warmer regions. They prefer sun and well-drained but moist soil.

A closely related species with the same common name of brass buttons (*Cotula coronopifolia*) looks similar, with yellow button flowers in summer. It will grow in water and is hardy in Zones 7 to 10.

CARE INSTRUCTIONS: Propagate by division in spring.

USES: Wet areas; between cracks and crevices of rock walls and pavers.

LIRIOPE

Lilyturf

- Hardiness varies
- Evergreen perennial
- 9 to 24 inches tall
- Space 8 to 12 inches
- Sun to partial shade
- Moderate to frequent watering

DESCRIPTION: Lilyturf forms fountain-spray-shaped clumps of straplike, shiny, dark evergreen leaves. In summer and fall, erect spikes bear small, inconspicuous, lavender or purple-blue flowers. As it is closely related to mondograss (*Ophiopogon*), the two plants are sometimes mistaken for each other.

Creeping lilyturf (*L. spicata*) grows to about 9 inches in height and is hardy to Zone 5. Its cultivar 'Silver Dragon' has green-and-white-striped leaves. Blue lilyturf (*L. muscari*) will reach heights of 1½ to 2 feet. Blooms are more noticeable on this species. Plants are hardy only to Zone 6.

Both lilyturf species prefer fertile, humus-rich soil that is moist but well-drained. They tolerate partial shade but flower best in a sunny site.

CARE INSTRUCTIONS: Protect plant foliage from windburn. Shear or mow them in late winter to remove spent foliage. Divide clumps every few years or when overcrowded. Propagate from seed sown in fall or by division in spring.

USES: As edging along paths and in mass plantings where you want a turf-like appearance; under trees.

'Variegata' lilyturf is a blue lilyturf that has creamy yellow leaf margins.

LONICERA

Honeysuckle

- Hardiness varies
- Evergreen to deciduous woody shrub or vine
- 2 feet tall
- Space 2 to 5 feet, depending on type
- Sun to partial shade
- Moderate watering

DESCRIPTION: There are about 180 honeysuckle varieties and species that range from evergreen to deciduous. They are treasured for their sweetly scented trumpet-shaped flowers and decorative fruit, which attracts birds. Some grow into large shrubs; others are vines that can be trained into ground covers.

Honeysuckle's wonderfully fragrant flowers appear from late winter or early spring to late summer. They range in color from cream and light yellow to vivid scarlet and purplish rose.

Most ground cover honeysuckles are aggressive vines that will rapidly cover an area if they have nothing to climb. They are wonderful on slopes and banks or other large, open places where there are no trees or shrubs that they might strangle. But take care where you plant them; they can be invasive. Space plants about 5 feet apart so they have plenty of room to ramble.

Trumpet honeysuckle (*L. sempervirens*) is among the most aggressive. Although it has a long bloom season, its flowers are pale; cultivars are much showier, including 'John Cayton' and 'Sulphurea', yellow flowers; 'Magnifica', 'Cedar Lane' and 'Superba' red blooms. Those of 'Cedar Lane' are 2 inches long.

Hall's honeysuckle (*L. japonica* 'Halliana') is evergreen to semi-evergreen in warm climates, deciduous in cold, and just as aggressive as trumpet honeysuckle. It has white flowers that fade to yellow in summer. Goldnet honeysuckle (*L. j.* 'Aureoreticulata') is less aggressive. Both are hardy to Zone 5 to 10.

Privet honeysuckle (*L. pileata*) is a semi-evergreen shrublike plant. It reaches 1 to 3 feet tall to about 3 feet in width. Purple berries follow small, fragrant white flowers, which bloom in midspring. It is hardy in Zones 8 to 10.

Space plants that you plan to grow as ground covers about 2 feet apart for maximum coverage. Honeysuckles prefer moist, loamy soil with lots of organic matter but can live in almost any well-drained soil. They tolerate shade but flower better if planted in plenty of sun.

CARE INSTRUCTIONS: Mulch to keep roots shaded and moist. Avoid manure mulches, which promote vegetative growth.

To make plants bushier, prune stem tips of young plants. Honeysuckles have a tendency to "roll over" on themselves with a trashy core of dead stems under the sparse foliage. Prune plants soon after they flower to keep the dead wood from building up, to prevent fruit from developing, and to maintain the plant's shape. Propagate from softwood cuttings taken in early summer. Problems: leaf curl; crown gall; powdery mildew.

USES: Slopes; open areas; erosion control.

Honeysuckle helps control erosion on slopes, especially in bright, sunny locales.

LYSIMACHIA

Loosestrife

Moneywort is a trailing plant that looks especially good in ponds and rock gardens.

- Hardy in Zones 3 to 10 (except desert)
- Evergreen perennial
- 2 to 4 inches tall
- Space 12 to 18 inches
- Partial to full shade
- Moderate to frequent watering

DESCRIPTION: Loosestrife species grow by stolons and can outgrow the boundaries of a bed. Moneywort (*L. nummularia*) is a trailing plant with crinkly or wavy leaves of greenish yellow. Plants bear large, yellow flowers on short stems in summer. 'Aurea' has yellow foliage. Minuite loosestrife (*L. japonica* 'Minuitissima') is a carpet-forming perennial with lime green leaves.

Single golden-yellow flowers punctuate the plant in summer. 'Echo Dark Satin' is available in the South and has red-throated yellow blossoms from spring to fall. It is a cultivar of dense-flowered loosestrife (*L. congestiflora*), with dark green leaves. 'Outback Sunset' is another dense-flowered loosestrife with similar blossoms and red-tinged, yellow-variegated leaves.

Plants grow best in moist, fertile, well-drained soil and partial shade.
CARE INSTRUCTIONS: Divide in spring or fall. Propagate from seed, divisions in spring or fall, and cuttings in spring or early summer.
USES: Water gardens; rock gardens; between stepping-stones.

MAHONIA

Grapeholly

Grapeholly is an attractive ground-cover accent for landscapes in cooler climates.

- Hardy in Zones 5 to 9
- Evergreen shrub
- Up to 2 feet tall
- Space 2 feet
- Partial to full shade
- Low to moderate watering

DESCRIPTION: Grapehollies have thick, leathery, spiny leaves that are dark blue-green in summer and turn rich purple-bronze in fall and winter. Creeping grapeholly (*M. repens*) is ideal for ground-cover use. It grows to about 2 feet in height and spreads 2 to 3 feet in width. These plants have clusters of yellow flowers during late spring and early summer, followed by dark blue berries in late summer to fall. The

yellow flowers particularly stand out against the dark foliage. Cascades mahonia (*M. nervosa*) has a similar appearance. It tolerates shadier sites and cooler climates. 'Compacta' Oregon grapeholly (*M. aquifolium*) has glossy leaves that turn bronze in winter. Plants grow as tall as 3 feet.

These plants do well in any well-drained soil and are drought-tolerant once established. They spread well on their own.
CARE INSTRUCTIONS: Shelter from winter sun and drying winds in cold regions. Propagate by cutting off suckers.
USES: Cool settings; accent plantings; interplanted with barberry.

MAZUS

Mazus

With its mat of bright green foliage and delicate flowers, mazus looks lovely amid pavers and rocks.

- Hardiness varies
- Evergreen to deciduous perennial
- 2 inches tall
- Space 6 to 12 inches
- Sun to partial shade
- Moderate to frequent watering

DESCRIPTION: These low-growing, spreading plants form mats of creeping foliage with bright green leaves. Most have small blue, lavender, or white flowers in spring that may be spotted with yellow. Creeping mazus (*M. reptans*) has lavender flowers spotted with yellow or white. It is evergreen in warm climates; elsewhere, it freezes to the ground in winter, recovering rapidly

in spring. It is hardy in Zones 4 to 10 (except in the desert). A white-flowered cultivar, 'Alba', is available. Japanese mazus (*M. japonicus*) grows slightly larger (2 to 4 inches tall) and has lighter green leaves and white flowers. It is hardy only to Zone 7.

Mazus plants grow well in average soil. They tolerate light foot traffic and can be invasive.
CARE INSTRUCTIONS: Provide a site with afternoon shade in regions with hot summers. Plants are relatively pest-free. Divide them every three to four years when they become overcrowded.
USES: Between rocks and pavers.

MENTHA

Mint

- Hardy in Zones 7 to 10
- Semi-evergreen perennial
- 1 to 3 feet tall
- Space 6 to 12 inches
- Sun to partial shade
- Moderate to frequent watering

DESCRIPTION: Some mints are used for culinary purposes, others in landscapes. All have a pungent aroma when crushed underfoot. Pennyroyal (M. *pulegium*) is a good ground-cover choice for cool climates. It has small dark green leaves and blue-lilac flowers in summer. Full sun and well-drained soil are best, but plants grow in light shade. For wet sites, in sun or partial shade, try water mint (M. *aquatica*), with dark green leaves on reddish stems and lilac colored blooms in summer. Plants can reach 3 feet tall, but they readily take shearing. Corsican mint (M. *requienii*) grows 1 inch tall in shade and moist soil. It has bright green leaves and a peppermint aroma. Tiny lavender flowers appear in summer. Plants tolerate foot traffic.

CARE INSTRUCTIONS: Shear or mow plants in winter before growth begins. Propagate pennyroyal and Corsican mint by seed or division in early spring, water mint from stem cuttings.

USES: Lightly traveled paths; beside streams and ponds.

Corsican mint is one of the shortest ground-cover mints; it releases a wonderful aroma when crushed.

MICROBIOTA DECUSSATA

Russian Cypress

- Hardy in Zones 2 to 10
- Evergreen coniferous shrub
- 20 inches tall
- Space 3 to 4 feet
- Sun to partial shade
- Moderate watering

DESCRIPTION: This low-growing conifer is a spreading shrub with flat sprays of leathery, scalelike leaves, almost like those of ground-cover junipers. The yellow-green leaves turn pinkish bronze in winter.

Russian cypress flowers are inconspicuous; they're followed by tiny globe-shaped, yellowish brown cones. One plant can spread as much as 9 to 12 feet in width.

This ground cover grows well in all soil types and can withstand drought. It also does well in shade, providing an effect similar to that of ground cover junipers, which do not take shade.

CARE INSTRUCTIONS: Shear annually to keep growth compact. Propagate from cuttings.

USES: Moderate to large areas; foundation plantings; substitute for juniper in shady sites.

As is the case with junipers, it takes only a few plants for Russian cypress to cover large areas.

MYOSOTIS

Forget-Me-Not

- Hardy in Zones 4 to 10
- Deciduous perennial
- 4 to 24 inches tall
- Space 6 to 12 inches
- Shade
- Moderate to frequent watering

DESCRIPTION: Forget-me-nots have dark green leaves and a profusion of tiny flowers in pink or blue in mid- to late spring.

True forget-me-not (M. *scorpioides*) loves moist soil and can be used near ponds and streams and in bog gardens. Woodland forget-me-not (M. *sylvatica*) does better in gardens where moisture is less consistent.

Forget-me-nots prefer fertile, sandy loam but do fine in most ordinary soil if it is well-drained.

CARE INSTRUCTIONS: Pinch the shoots of these plants to encourage bushier growth. Forget-me-nots self-seed well. Propagate them from seed in fall or early spring or by division or stem cuttings in spring or summer.

USES: Wet areas; rock gardens; moist banks.

Forget-me-nots add color and lushness to moist, shaded areas.

OPHIOPOGON

Mondograss

Mondograss is sometimes confused with liriope, but its leaves are much finer-textured.

- Hardy in Zones 7 to 10
- Evergreen perennial
- 6 to 12 inches tall
- Space 6 to 8 inches
- Sun to partial shade
- Moderate to frequent watering

DESCRIPTION: These ground covers are not true grasses, but grow in a tuft resembling a grass.

Mondograss (*O. japonicus*) is a spreading plant that grows about a foot high. It has slender, shiny, dark evergreen leaves and small, tubular, lilac-colored flowers on spikelike stalks in late summer. Small, blue, pea-size fruit resembling berries follow the blooms.

Black mondograss (*O. planiscapus* 'Nigrescens') forms clumps of purple-black foliage up to 9 inches tall with a spread of 12 inches or more. It has linear, evergreen leaves and upright clusters of small, tubular white or lilac flowers and small, dull blue, pea-size fruit.

Mondograss prefers fertile, moist, humus-rich, well-drained soil and can be grown in sun or light shade.
CARE INSTRUCTIONS: Mow or cut it back in spring before new growth begins. In full sun, mondograss needs more frequent watering. Propagate by division.
USES: Borders; mass plantings.

OSTEOSPERMUM FRUTICOSUM

African Daisy

African daisies, also called freeway daisies, are showy ground covers with year-round blooms.

- Hardy in Zones 8 to 10 (West, except desert)
- Evergreen perennial
- Up to 2 feet tall
- Space 2 feet
- Sun
- Moderate watering

DESCRIPTION: Called the freeway daisy in the West, the species *O. fruticosum* can cover a 2- to 4-foot area in a year. It has daisylike flowers, lilac fading to white on top and darker below with a dark purple center. Plants bloom all year, but most heavily in winter. *O. jucundum* displays single, soft pink daisies. Many showy hybrids are available. 'Whirligig' has dark gray-green,

coarse-textured leaves. Large single daisies with spoon-shaped petals appear in summer. Petals are white above and light blue or gray below and pinched or rolled up so both colors show. Centers are dark blue-gray. 'Buttermilk' produces pale yellow flowers with dark reddish brown centers in summer.

African daisies prefer fertile, well-drained soil in full sun. They are hardy only in frost-free areas.
CARE INSTRUCTIONS: Cut plants back to healthy new growth after flowering has ceased. Propagate from seed or cuttings in midsummer.
USES: Seashore and hot inland areas, but not desert.

PACHYSANDRA

Pachysandra

Pachysandra thrives under trees and controls erosion on shady slopes.

- Hardiness varies
- Evergreen woody shrub
- 8 inches tall
- Space 12 inches
- Shade
- Moderate to frequent watering

DESCRIPTION: Pachysandra is one of the most common ground covers. It forms underground runners that mat in the soil. Japanese spurge (*P. terminalis*) is evergreen in all regions. It grows upright with medium to dark green coarse-textured leaves in whorls at the tips. Small, inconspicuous white flowers appear in late spring. 'Variegata' has silver-edged leaves; the leaves of 'Green Sheen' are lustrous dark

green. Plants are hardy in Zones 4 to 9 (except in desert regions).

Allegheny spurge (*P. procumbens*) is evergreen in warm regions, deciduous in areas cooler than Zone 7. Its foliage is attractively mottled with gray to blue green, and it has pinkish white to purple flowers in spring.

Plants prefer shady areas (foliage turns yellow with too much sun) and do well in ordinary, slightly acid soil. Pachysandra does not tolerate foot traffic and is not drought- or heat-tolerant.
CARE INSTRUCTIONS: Apply fertilizer each spring. Propagate by division. Problem: fungal diseases.
USES: Under trees; erosion control.

PELARGONIUM PELTATUM

Ivy Geranium

- Hardy in Zones 9 and 10
- Evergreen shrub
- 4 to 24 inches tall
- Space 18 to 24 inches
- Sun to partial shade
- Moderate to frequent watering

DESCRIPTION: Plants have ivy-shaped leaves and trailing stems with single or double flowers in crimson, scarlet, salmon-pink, pale pink, and white. Flowers form in dense clusters on strong stalks like those of garden geraniums. Leaf colors include bicolor, tricolor, and quadricolor, with combinations of purple, pink, cream, white, orange, yellow, bronze, red, or coppery red. The round, long-stemmed leaves may be wavy or lobed. Stems, though soft and flexible, are woody at the base. The entire plant is coated with soft, fine fuzz.

Ivy geranium does well in a wide variety of soils and in full sun or partial shade.

CARE INSTRUCTIONS: Trim plants once in autumn or occasionally throughout the growing season. Protect them from hard frosts. Propagate from cuttings taken in August and September, by seed, or division.

USES: Walls; slopes.

With its tumbling growth habit and lovely flowers, ivy geranium trails over walls and on slopes.

PHLOX

Phlox

- Hardy in Zones 3 to 10
- Herbaceous evergreen shrub or perennial
- 6 to 24 inches
- Space 12 to 18 inches
- Sun to partial shade
- Low to moderate watering

DESCRIPTION: Phlox has vivid, bright blooms (phlox means flame). Some grow quite tall, but dwarf perennial phlox makes lovely ground covers. Wild sweet William (*P. divaricata* 'Fullers White') is 8 to 12 inches tall, with creamy white flowers. Wild sweet William is native to woodlands and has an erect growth habit. At 12 to 15 inches tall, it forms large flowers on loose heads in May and June that are lavender-blue and lightly scented. Moss phlox (*P. subulata*) grows 6 to 8 inches tall, spreads to 2 feet wide, and has sharp-pointed leaves. Its cultivars have red, pink, white, or lavender flowers.

Phlox prefers full sun and well-drained, sandy, moist to somewhat dry soil. Wild sweet William does well in light loam and leaf mold in partial shade in the rock garden. Moss phlox grows well in full sun.

CARE INSTRUCTIONS: Propagate from seed or cuttings taken during spring and summer, or by root division in spring or early summer.

USES: Edging walkways.

Phlox forms wide-spreading mats in full sun. This is the cultivar 'Marjorie'.

PHYLA NODIFLORA

Lippia

- Hardy in Zones 9 and 10
- Evergreen perennial
- 2 inches tall
- Space 12 to 24 inches
- Sun
- Moderate watering

DESCRIPTION: Plants have oval gray-green leaves on creeping stems. The foliage forms a dense mat that is about 2 inches tall. In shade, plants can reach 6 inches tall. Tiny pink or lavender flowers appear from spring through summer. The blooms are held above the foliage. Its creeping growth habit and ability to withstand foot traffic make lippia a good lawn alternative. However, its flowers attract bees, which can be troublesome to some people.

Lippia grows in a wide range of soil types. Although it does best in full sun, it will grow in partial shade. Plants withstand extreme heat and are drought-resistant.

CARE INSTRUCTIONS: Mow to suppress flower formation. Fertilize in early spring. Propagate by division, planting small pieces of "sod" 4 inches apart. Problem: nematodes.

USES: Between pavers; lawn alternative; desert gardens.

Sun-loving lippia makes a fine lawn substitute and is suited to desert gardens.

POTENTILLA
Cinquefoil

Cinquefoils come in many shapes and sizes, from this shrubby variety to more herbaceous, clumping types.

- Hardy in Zones 5 to 9
- Perennial or shrub
- Up to 3 feet tall
- Space 1 foot
- Sun to partial shade
- Moderate watering

DESCRIPTION: *Potentilla* includes hardy, clump-forming and creeping perennials and shrubs. Plants vary in height from 8 to 24 inches to 3 feet and have attractive foliage and saucer-shaped, roselike flowers. 'Miss Willmott' (*P. nepalensis*) forms sprawling clumps of green. Cup-shaped pink flowers with cherry-red centers top plants in summer. 'Gibson's Scarlet' (*P. atrosanguinea*) has dark green, strawberry-like leaves and bright scarlet flowers in summer. The leaves of *P. megalantha* are large, pale green, and downy. An abundance of rich yellow flowers cover plants during summer. Shrubby or bush cinquefoil (*P. fruticosa*) grows 2 to 3 feet tall and has large yellow flowers all summer.

Cinquefoils prefer moderately fertile, cool, moist but well-drained soil and will die in winter if planted in heavy, wet clay soil.

CARE INSTRUCTIONS: Propagate by seed or division in spring or fall. Shrubs are propagated in late summer by taking hardwood cuttings.

USES: Borders; slopes; rock gardens.

ROSA
Rose

Ground cover roses, such as this pink Flower Carpet rose, do well as barriers and on slopes and banks.

- Hardy in Zones 4 to 10
- Evergreen to deciduous shrub
- Up to 2½ feet tall
- Space 8 to 10 feet
- Sun
- Moderate to frequent watering

DESCRIPTION: Ground-cover roses include vigorous, disease-resistant, hardy plants that spread up to 8 feet wide. Most bloom throughout the growing season. The Flower Carpet series has massive clusters of slightly fragrant blooms in pink, white, red, and yellow on strong, arching stems. Meidiland landscape roses include 'Fire Meidiland' (2 inches tall by 4 feet wide, fire-engine red blooms); 'Alba Meidiland' (white flowers, 2 to 2½ feet tall and 4 feet wide); 'White Meidiland' (also white flowers, 1½ to 2 feet tall by 4 to 5 feet wide); and 'Magic Meidiland' (pink flowers, 2 feet tall and 5 feet wide).

Roses need at least six hours of sun a day and regular to fertile, slightly acid, well-drained soil.

CARE INSTRUCTIONS: Thin dead or overcrowded branches in winter or early spring, when the hips (fruit) are gone. Fertilize plants annually. Mulch to suppress diseases and weeds and to retain water in soil. Propagate by cuttings taken in summer or by layering.

USES: Barrier plants; on walls and other structures; slopes and banks.

ROSMARINUS OFFICINALIS
Trailing Rosemary

Trailing rosemary is a fragrant, evergreen shrub that does well in dry, drought-prone sites.

- Hardy in Zones 8 to 10
- Evergreen shrub
- Up to 2 feet tall
- Space 2 feet
- Sun
- Low to moderate watering

DESCRIPTION: Trailing rosemary is a fragrant evergreen shrub—the same plant grown as an herb. For ground-cover use, look for creeping forms that grow low to the ground and require less trimming to control growth. These include 'Huntington Carpet', which is 1 to 2 feet tall and spreads to 8 feet, and 'Prostratus', at 8 to 24 inches in height. In early summer, rosemary produces small two-lipped flowers of blue, white, or lilac that form on leaf axils all along the stem.

Plants thrive in dry, rocky, limy or alkaline, well-drained soil in sunny locations. Rosemary is more susceptible to damage in harsh winter weather if it is planted in heavy clay soil. In extremely cold climates, grow plants in a protected area.

CARE INSTRUCTIONS: The plant is drought-tolerant, but water occasionally in dry periods. Prune annually as soon as flowers fade. Propagate rosemary from cuttings made in late summer or early fall, or from seed.

USES: Coastal and dry settings; slopes; over walls.

SANTOLINA CHAMAECYPARISSUS

Lavender Cotton

- Hardy in Zones 6 to 10
- Evergreen shrub to herbaceous perennial
- Up to 2½ feet tall
- Space 3 feet
- Sun
- Moderate watering

DESCRIPTION: Lavender cotton grows with fine-textured, grayish green, aromatic leaves and bright yellow, buttonlike flowers. Flowers appear in summer and last at least a month. Long stems billow out from the trunk, but plants can be sheared for a more compact appearance. Green lavender cotton (*S. rosmarinifolia*) has bright green needle-like leaves and creamy light green flowers (Zone 7).

Lavender cotton grows well in a wide range of climates and soil types. Plants are drought-tolerant once they are established. They are also salt-tolerant, so they grow well in desert areas.

CARE INSTRUCTIONS: Older plants may become woody or shabby. Prune plants yearly to within a foot of the ground in early spring. Propagate from stem cuttings in spring or fall.

USES: Low hedges.

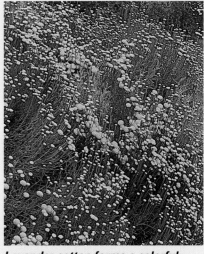

Lavender cotton forms a colorful, aromatic ground cover.

SAXIFRAGA STOLONIFERA

Strawberry Geranium

- Most are hardy in Zones 7 to 10 (except desert)
- Evergreen perennial
- 5 to 24 inches tall
- Space 12 to 18 inches
- Partial to full shade
- Frequent watering

DESCRIPTION: *Saxifraga* includes a large group of hardy perennials native to temperate and arctic regions. Gardeners may be most familiar with the species as a houseplant, but strawberry geranium grows outdoors as well.

It forms mats of rounded, silver-patterned, hairy leaves, which are red underneath. Plants spread by long, strawberry-like runners. Airy spikes of white flowers rise above the plants on 2-foot stems. Leaves and flower stems of 'Maroon Beauty' are covered in red hairs (it is reportedly hardy to Zone 3). 'Tricolor' has creamy white leaf margins.

Many other and hardier saxifragas are available. They're typically used in rock gardens, and some have earned a reputation for being temperamental. Strawberry geranium does fine as long as it has moist, well-drained soil and part shade.

CARE INSTRUCTIONS: Propagate from seed, cuttings, or division.

USES: Interplanting.

Strawberry geranium, ideal for southern climates, has a wide range of growth habits.

SEDUM

Sedum

- Hardy in Zones 4 to 10
- Evergreen succulent perennial
- 2 to 9 inches tall
- Space 12 inches
- Sun to partial shade
- Moderate watering

DESCRIPTION: Dozens of ground-cover sedums are available. All offer interesting foliage as well as showy, star-shaped blooms. Goldmoss stonecrop (*S. acre*) has tiny, mosslike leaves; it grows 2 to 3 inches tall with yellow flowers in spring. Two-row stonecrop (*S. spurium*) is 2 to 6 inches tall with white to rose flowers in summer. 'Dragon's Blood' has red leaves and rosy flowers. Kamschatka stonecrop (*S. kamtschaticum*) is a little taller, at 4 to 9 inches; its flat-headed yellow flowers appear in summer along with large, toothed leaves.

Plants grow best in fertile, well-drained soil and full sun but take partial shade. Plants sometimes propagate themselves from leaves that break off.

CARE INSTRUCTIONS: Water occasionally in summer. Propagate plants by division in spring or by cuttings.

USES: Between rocks and pavers; cover for small areas; as firebreak.

Sedums are succulent plants that work well as firebreaks and to fill spaces between rocks and pavers.

SEMPERVIVUM

Hen and Chicks

Houseleeks are highly adaptable succulents for dry, sunny or partly shaded sites, such as under trees.

- Hardy in Zones 4 to 10
- Perennial evergreen succulent
- 1 to 4 inches tall
- Space 6 to 8 inches
- Sun to partial shade
- Low to moderate watering

DESCRIPTION: Hen and checks, sometimes called houseleeks, form ground-hugging rosettes of tough, succulent leaves. The rosettes may be 6 inches in diameter. Clusters of red, purple, white, or yellow flowers rise above foliage on 15-inch stems. *S. tectorum* is one of the most common species, and many cultivars are available. 'Atropurpureum' has dark violet leaves. Leaves of 'Royanum' are yellow-green tipped with red; 'Sunset' has orange-red leaves; 'Triste' has reddish brown. *S. calcareum* is similar to *S. tectorum* except it has broader leaves tipped with reddish brown. Cobweb hen and chicks (*S. arachnoideum*) has "cobweb"-connected leaf tips and bright red flowers in July.

Hen and chicks are adaptable to most soils, even infertile ones, as long as the site is well-drained. They are tolerant of drought.
CARE INSTRUCTIONS: Water occasionally in the heat of summer. Remove dead rosettes to make room for new growth. Propagate from seed and division, separating offshoots.
USES: Rock gardens; gentle, dry slopes; under trees.

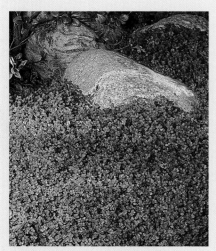

Baby's tears are delicate, fast-spreading ground covers in areas protected from foot traffic.

SOLEIROLIA SOLEIROLII

Baby's Tears

- Hardy in Zones 9 and 10
- Herbaceous evergreen perennial
- Up to 3 inches tall
- Space 12 inches
- Shade
- Frequent watering

DESCRIPTION: This tender, fast-growing creeping perennial forms tight mats of round, emerald- or chartreuse-colored leaves and interlacing stems that create a soft 1- to 3-inch-tall carpet. The foliage is composed of tiny, rounded leaves. Plants spread rapidly, so they can cover shady areas quickly, but may become invasive.

Baby's tears requires shade, rich soil, and moisture. Plants are readily killed by direct sun, drought, and freezing temperatures.
CARE INSTRUCTIONS: Protect from foot traffic and hard frosts. Stepping on the plants causes damage to the tender foliage that is visible for days. Propagate baby's tears by division.
USES: At the base of trees and shade plants, such as ferns.

STACHYS BYZANTINA

Lamb's Ears

The soft, silvery, fuzzy leaves of lamb's ears contrast well with dark-colored ground covers.

- Hardy in Zones 4 to 10
- Herbaceous evergreen or deciduous perennial
- 12 to 18 inches tall
- Space 18 inches
- Sun
- Moderate watering

DESCRIPTION: The soft, thick leaves are densely covered in white fuzz, which makes them look silvery. Pink or purple flowers appear on woolly spikes in summer. 'Primrose Heron' has leaves that emerge yellowish green, then become silvery, and erect spikes of small, tubular, pink summer flowers. 'Silver Carpet' forms a 6-inch-thick carpet of white woolly leaves; it rarely flowers. 'Big Ears' (also called 'Countess Helene von Stein') is a nonflowering variety with sturdy foliage. Another species, big betony (*S. macrantha* 'Superba') forms ground-hugging clumps of heart-shaped, crinkled, medium green leaves. Dense, whorled spikes of purplish violet bloom in midsummer on 1- to 2-foot stems.

Plants flourish in average, well-drained, sandy soil in sunny spots.
CARE INSTRUCTIONS: Rhizomes spread rapidly. Cut flower stalks after flowering. Divide plants if overcrowded. Remove winter-damaged foliage. Propagate by seed, division, or cuttings.
USES: Small mass plantings; accents.

TEUCRIUM CHAMAEDRYS

Wall Germander

- Hardy in Zones 6 to 10
- Evergreen shrubby perennial
- 8 to 24 inches tall
- Space 18 to 24 inches
- Sun to partial shade
- Low to moderate watering

DESCRIPTION: Wall germander has shiny green leaves and bell-shaped, tubular flowers in pink or purple that appear summer to fall. Growth is rapid by spreading underground root systems. 'Nanum' is a dwarf cultivar. 'Variegatum' has leaves variegated with creamy markings. 'Prostratum' is a ground-hugging cultivar.

Plants grow best in any well-drained soil and full sun, but they tolerate and even thrive in sun, heat, and poor, rocky soil. They are also drought-tolerant and easy to maintain once established.

CARE INSTRUCTIONS: Only occasional watering is needed in summer; don't overwater. Shear straggly plants to encourage bushier, more compact growth. Although plants tolerate heavy pruning, they are weakened by it. Propagate by seed or terminal cuttings.

USES: Edging; dwarf hedges; rock gardens; low-maintenance sites; hot or dry settings.

Wall germanders add grace and beauty to poor, rocky, hot or dry landscapes.

THYMUS

Thyme

- Hardy in Zones 5 to 10
- Evergreen perennial
- 4 to 12 inches tall
- Space 12 inches
- Sun to partial shade
- Moderate watering

DESCRIPTION: Ground-cover varieties of this herb are prostrate or creeping and have tiny leaves and small but colorful flowers. All release a delightful scent when walked on. Lemon thyme (*T. × citriodorus*) grows 8 to 12 inches tall and 2 feet wide. The lemon-scented leaves are glossy and dark green; pale lilac flowers appear in summer. Wild thyme (*T. serpyllum*) has tiny dark green leaves and purple flowers in June on 3- to 6-inch-tall plants. Silvery gray thyme (*T. pseudolanuginosus*) is 2 to 3 inches tall with gray, fuzzy leaves and lilac colored flowers. Caraway thyme (*T. herba-barona*) resembles creeping thyme, with thicker, larger, fleshier leaves. It has lilac hued flowers and a caraway scent.

Thymes prefer well-drained, dry soil with a pH of 6.5 to 7.5 and full sun. They will take partial shade.

CARE INSTRUCTIONS: Water regularly in hot weather. Divide plants every three to five years. After flowering, nip branch tips. Propagate from seed sown indoors in early spring and by cuttings. Problems: fungal, foliage diseases.

USES: Between pavers and stepping-stones; dry sites.

This red-flowering thyme adds fragrance and color to a hot, dry site.

TRACHELOSPERMUM

Star Jasmine

- Hardy in Zones 8 to 10
- Evergreen vine
- 1 to 2 feet tall
- Space 3 feet
- Sun to partial shade
- Frequent watering

DESCRIPTION: Handsome star jasmine (*T. jasminoides*) is a twining rambler with woody stems that grow 30 feet long. Glossy, leathery, oval leaves are light green when young and become darker green as they age. Fragrant white, pinwheel-shaped flowers appear in summer. Asiatic jasmine (*T. asiaticum*) is a similar plant with smaller, duller leaves and yellow or cream flowers.

Both plants are slow to get started but are quite sturdy once established. They do well in average, well-drained soil and need some shade if grown in particularly hot locales or in desert settings.

CARE INSTRUCTIONS: Fertilize at the beginning of the growing season and again after flowering. If signs of chlorosis appear (which is possible in alkaline soil), apply iron chelate or iron sulfate. Cut back upright stems. Propagate by stem cuttings.

USES: Slopes; over walls; under trees.

Star jasmine is a southern vine that looks wonderful draping and trailing over slopes and walls.

VACCINIUM

Blueberry and Mountain Cranberry

Mountain cranberry produces small, edible fruit. Its leathery leaves turn red-bronze in winter.

- Hardy in Zones 2 to 6
- Deciduous to evergreen shrub
- 6 to 24 inches tall
- Space 12 inches
- Sun to partial shade
- Moderate to frequent watering

DESCRIPTION: There are a number of low-growing, woody shrubs in this genus. Mountain cranberry (*V. vitis-idaea minus*) spreads 2 or more feet across. Its oval, leathery, evergreen leaves are glossy dark green on top and spotted below. In mid- to late spring, drooping spikes of white or pinkish, bell-shaped flowers appear with small, edible, berrylike red fruit in August. Lowbush blueberry (*V. augustifolium*) is a deciduous shrub with lustrous dark blue-green leaves turning scarlet in fall. Its tiny, red-tinged-white, urn-shaped spring blooms are followed by sweet, dark blue, fruit in mid- to late summer. Creeping blueberry (*V. crassifolium*) is similar to mountain cranberry but hardy only to Zone 8.

Plants prefer acid soil high in organic matter. A pH range of 4.5 to 5.5 is best.

CARE INSTRUCTIONS: Give plants plenty of moisture. Propagate by seed, cuttings, or division. Problems: dieback; leaf spot; viral ring spot; scale; stem borers; stem gall (caused by wasps); tent caterpillars.

USES: Small areas; naturalized settings; rock gardens.

VANCOUVERIA

American Barrenwort

Barrenwort looks especially lovely in naturalized settings.

- Hardy in Zones 5 to 8
- Deciduous to evergreen perennial
- 7 to 18 inches tall
- Space 10 to 14 inches
- Moderate to deep shade
- Moderate to frequent watering

DESCRIPTION: With its lobed, slender-stalked, blue-green leaves and panicles of small, drooping flowers, which rise above the foliage, *Vancouveria* species resemble *Epimediums*. American barrenwort (*V. hexandra*) is a deciduous perennial that grows to about 18 inches tall. White flowers appear in mid- to late spring.

Inside-out-flower (*V. planipetala*) is an evergreen species with light to medium green leaves. It grows 7 to 12 inches tall and has tiny white or lavender-tinged flowers in mid- to late spring. *V. chrysantha* blooms in yellow. It is evergreen, but less hardy than inside-out-flower (Zone 6).

Barrenworts do best in humus-rich, acid, well-drained, loamy soil. They like cool, moist conditions.

CARE INSTRUCTIONS: Topdress plants annually with compost. Keep the soil moist because these plants are not drought-tolerant. Propagate them by division in spring or fall.

USES: Naturalized settings; companion plants for ferns, azaleas, and rhododendrons.

VERONICA

Speedwells

'Trehane' prostrate speedwell grows 8 inches tall and has yellow-green foliage.

- Hardiness varies
- Perennial
- 4 to 8 inches tall
- Space 12 inches
- Sun to partial shade
- Frequent watering

DESCRIPTION: Speedwells are vigorous, fast-growing plants with spiky white, pink, blue, or purple flowers in summer. They are deciduous in the North and can be evergreen in the South.

Fastest- and lowest-growing species include prostrate speedwell (*V. prostrata*), 6 inches tall, dark green leaves, Zone 5; silver speedwell (*V. incana*), 6 inches tall, gray-green leaves, neat blue spikes on long stalks, Zone 3; and creeping speedwell (*V. repens*), 4 inches tall, dark leaves, small blue flowers, Zone 6.

Speedwells prefer slightly acid, well-drained soil. Some make fine lawn alternatives where there is no foot traffic; some may be invasive.

CARE INSTRUCTIONS: Shear or mow to remove spent flowers. Take care when fertilizing; leaves burn easily. Propagate from seed, cuttings, or division. Problems: downy mildew; leaf spot; leaf gall; root rot; leaf smut; Japanese weevil; southern root knot nematodes.

USES: Rock gardens; path edges. Prostrate varieties: between paving stones; large areas.

Vines

■ FIVELEAF AKEBIA:

Fiveleaf akebia (*Akebia quinata*) is a vigorous deciduous to evergreen woody climber that grows 28 to 40 feet up but will stay close to the ground if draped over the soil. Its glossy leaves are composed of five leaflets tinged with red. Fragrant reddish purple flowers appear in mid-spring, if the weather is mild, followed in long, hot summers by dark purple, 2- to 4-inch-long fruit. The vine has both male and female plants, and only the females fruit.

Akebias thrive in light, well-drained soil in sun or partial shade. Space them 3 to 4 feet apart and water moderately. Do not plant them near low-growing shrubs that they might overtake. Trim excessively long shoots in late fall or early spring. Propagate akebia from seed, layering, or cuttings. Hardy in Zones 4 to 10 but highly invasive in mild climates.

■ WOOD VAMP:

Wood vamp (*Decumaria barbara*) is a semi-evergreen or evergreen vine. It climbs 30 feet high by aerial roots, but it can be trained as a ground cover. When it is trailing over the ground, its leaves stand about 6 inches tall. In early to midsummer, small, white, honey-scented flowers cover the plants.

Grow wood vamp in full sun, spaced 3 feet apart. Water moderately and prune after flowering. Propagate by semi-hardwood cuttings. Hardy in Zones 6 to 10.

■ BLOOD-RED TRUMPET VINE:

Blood-red trumpet vine (*Distictis buccinatoria*) forms a 2-foot-tall ground cover. Plants bloom throughout spring, summer, and fall (when the weather is warm). The trumpet-shaped flowers are orange-red with purple-red to yellow throats; they grow in clusters. The plants' shiny foliage is evergreen in mild climates, semi-evergreen elsewhere.

Plants need full sun, well-amended, fertile soil, and constant moisture, but with care they will do well in desert heat. Space them 3 feet apart. Thin to control growth and prevent tangling. Remove dead twigs. Hardy in Zones 9 to 10.

■ CLIMBING HYDRANGEA:

Climbing hydrangea (*Hydrangea petiolaris*) is a massive, deciduous to evergreen woody vine with large clusters of creamy flowers in midsummer. As a ground cover, it forms 2-foot-tall mounds.

Plants grow best in loamy, humus-rich, well-drained, acid soil and shade. Space them 3 feet apart and mulch to keep roots moist. Protect plants from spring frosts. Prune in late winter or early spring. Propagate climbing hydrangea from cuttings in April to August.

Hardy in Zones 5 to 10. A related species, *H. serratifolia*, has small leathery leaves and long panicles of cream-colored flowers. It is hardy to Zone 8.

■ VIRGINIA CREEPER:

Virginia creeper (*Parthenocissus quinquefolia*) is a versatile, deciduous, woody vine, tolerant of both cold and heat. It has five-part dark green leaves that turn bright red in fall. Its flowers are small and inconspicuous, but they are followed by clusters of dark purple berries in early fall. Birds love the fruit, so you may never see it.

Plants climb any upright surface they come across via tendrils and sticky disks that cling to surfaces, but well-trimmed plants will trail across the soil surface as a 1-foot-tall ground cover. There is a western form (*P. inserta*) with similar growth habits but without sticky disks, so it sprawls rather than climbs.

Virginia creepers can be grown in full sun to shade. Space them 3 feet apart and mow every few years. These plants do well in almost any soil type as long as they get plenty of water. Problems: leaf spot; Japanese beetles; spider mites. Hardy in Zones 4 to 10.

Trained to stay on the ground, climbing hydrangea is a clinging vine that makes a fine ground cover in shade.

Virginia creeper is a woody vine that may climb or sprawl depending on the variety.

■ BLUE PASSIONFLOWER:

Passionflowers (*Passiflora* spp.) encompass a variety of evergreen and deciduous climbing plants with tendrils. They can grow 20 to 30 feet high, but if allowed to trail and mound, they make a 2-foot-high ground cover. All have large, tubular flowers with showy stamens. Colors range from white to bluish purple to rose-red to violet-mauve. Some produce colorful, showy, edible fruit.

Plants prefer sunny locations in well-drained, loamy soil. Space them 2 to 3 feet apart and water moderately. Prune in spring and pinch back new shoots throughout the growing season so plants keep their shape. Passionflowers can be invasive in mild climates. Propagate from seed sown in spring or summer and softwood cuttings taken in early summer. Hardy in Zones 8 to 10.

VINCA

Vinca

Vinca, also known as periwinkle, does well in a wide range of conditions.

- Hardiness varies
- Evergreen perennial
- 6 to 12 inches tall
- Space 18 inches
- Sun to shade
- Moderate watering

DESCRIPTION: Vinca has spreading or arching stems that bear pairs of shiny, oval, dark green leaves. Its showy, five-petaled white, blue, or lavender flowers herald spring.

Large vinca (*V. major*) has the larger leaves and flowers (2 inches across), and forms a 1- to 2-foot-tall ground cover; it is hardy in Zones 7 to 10. 'Variegata' is irregularly marked with creamy white. Dwarf vinca (*V. minor*) is a small version, but its growth habit is more prostrate; plants grow to 6 inches tall. Plants also have narrower leaves and smaller flowers, to 1-inch across. This species is hardy in Zones 5 to 7.

Vincas root from stems anywhere they touch the ground. Plants grow best in light shade and good, moist, well-drained soil. Dwarf vinca is not suited to hot, desert areas. They compete well with the roots of other plants, including trees.

CARE INSTRUCTIONS: If plants mound too high, shear or mow in winter. Propagate by division or stem or root cuttings. Problems: blight; canker; dieback; leaf spot; root rot.

USES: Under trees.

Wedelia is a trailing plant that can handle the conditions along the seashore and in low desert areas.

WEDELIA TRILOBATA

Wedelia

- Hardy in Zones 9 and 10
- Evergreen perennial
- 4 to 18 inches tall
- Space 18 inches
- Sun to shade
- Frequent watering

DESCRIPTION: This trailing plant has fleshy glossy, three-part evergreen leaves that form a lush mat. For most of the year, it is dotted with 1-inch-diameter yellow flowers that look like small zinnia-like blooms.

Plants spread rapidly and root wherever the creeping stems touch the ground. The plants are easily killed by frosts.

Wedelia is unusual in that plants will grow in both boggy and desert settings. They tolerate wet and dry, sand and clay, acid and alkaline soils. Because the plants have good salt tolerance, they're especially suited to desert regions.

CARE INSTRUCTIONS: Shear or mow plants to improve appearance and to keep foliage at a uniform height. Propagate from stem tip cuttings or division.

USES: Seashores; low desert areas; bank stabilization.

Yellow-root can beautify the edges of streams and ponds in sun or dense shade.

XANTHORHIZA SIMPLICISSIMA

Yellow-Root

- Hardy in Zones 5 to 8
- Deciduous woody shrub
- 2 feet tall
- Space 18 to 24 inches
- Sun to dense shade
- Moderate watering

DESCRIPTION: Yellow-root is an easy-to-grow deciduous shrub, forming a uniform 2-foot-tall ground cover. Its oval to oblong leaves turn a beautiful yellow-orange in autumn. In spring, drooping clusters of tiny brownish purple, star-shaped flowers on long spikes appear before leaves unfold.

Plants tolerate a wide range of soils, but they grow most luxuriantly in humus-rich, moist but well-drained soil with a pH of 4.5 to 6. Part to full shade is also best for the plants. They withstand wet conditions and clay soil.

CARE INSTRUCTIONS: Shear plants in early spring to promote lateral branching. Propagate by cuttings or division.

USES: Stream banks, beside ponds, or in other wet areas; edging; under trees.

SHRUBBY GROUND COVER CULTIVARS

■ GLOSSY ABELIA:

Most glossy abelias *(Abelia × grandiflora)* grow 8 feet tall, but a few cultivars make ideal ground covers. 'Prostrata' and 'Sherwoodii' grow only 2 feet tall but spread up to 5 feet.

Plants have finely textured, glossy, bright green to bronze semi-evergreen leaves. From midsummer to midfall, clusters of small waxy, bell-shaped, fragrant flowers in white, pink, and lavender cover the plants. In winter, leaves are purplish.

Abelias grow in average soil but prefer well-drained loam and regular watering. Although they will grow in partial shade, full sun is best. Space plants 18 to 36 inches apart. Prune in spring to remove old, dead, or weak branches. Propagate from seed or cuttings or by layering. Hardy in Zones 6 to 10.

■ BARBERRY:

Barberries *(Berberis thunbergii)* are tough plants, enduring polluted air in industrial areas, cities, and roadsides. They typically reach 5 feet tall, but several 2-foot cultivars are available. 'Kobold', with bright green deciduous leaves, grows into a perfect mound at maturity. Leaves of 'Atropurpurea Nana' are red; plants broaden slowly, about 5 inches per year. You may also find this cultivar sold as 'Crimson Pygmy'. Bright yellow foliage and red berries mark 'Bonanza Gold'.

Plants grow best in well-drained soil and full sun. In very hot areas, they do better with afternoon shade. Space plants 6 feet apart. Most ground-cover barberries rarely need pruning; they grow in tight mounds. Propagate plants from seed sown in early spring, from July or August cuttings, or from suckers. In some areas, it is illegal to grow barberries because they are an alternate host to wheat rust diseases. Hardy in Zones 5 to 10.

■ HEAVENLY BAMBOO:

The common name of heavenly bamboo *(Nandina domestica)* arises from its bamboo-like stems and finely textured foliage. Leaves open with a light pink or coppery tint, turn green in summer, then bronze, orange, red, or purple in fall and winter. Large clusters of white flowers appear in summer, followed by red to white berries from fall to spring. Dwarf varieties include 'Harbor Dwarf', a dense, 1½- to 2-foot-tall mound with reddish purple winter color; 'Firepower', bright red winter leaves; and 'Moon Bay', light green in summer, red in winter.

Grow heavenly bamboo in full sun to shade (colors are brightest in sun) and moist, rich soil. It tolerates average soil and drought. Space plants 12 to 18 inches apart. Prune old stems to the ground. Plants are relatively pest-free and easy to maintain. Hardy in Zones 7 to 10.

Heavenly bamboo foliage opens with a pink tint, changes to green, then to bronze or orange in fall.

■ INDIAN HAWTHORN:

An evergreen lovely for mass planting, low hedges, or foundation plantings, Indian hawthorn *(Rhaphiolepis indica)* has clusters of fragrant pink or white flowers in spring. Small blue berries follow in late summer. Ground-cover cultivars include *R. indica* 'Pink Dancer', which reaches 16 inches tall by 3 feet wide with deep pink blooms and red foliage over winter; and 'Coates Crimson', which has blooms of crimson-pink.

Plant Indian hawthorn in ordinary soil and full sun, spacing plants 3 to 5 feet apart. Provide moderate amounts of water; plants do not tolerate drought. Prune and shape after flowering. Propagate from summer cuttings. Hardy in Zones 8 to 10.

Ground-cover barberries offer diverse choices in foliage color, from bright yellow-green to dark reddish brown. This is 'Atropurpurea Nana'.

■ RASPBERRY:

Several raspberry species *(Rubus spp.)* make good-looking ground covers. Nepalese raspberry *(R. nepalensis)* is 4 inches tall, spreads into a carpet of foliage, and produces edible fruit from late July to September. Creeping raspberry *(R. pentalobus)* grows to 4 inches tall; it has rough, thick-textured leaves. 'Emerald Carpet' is an improved cultivar with raspberry-colored leaves in winter.

Raspberries require well-drained soil and full sun. They can take some shade in hotter climates. Space plants 3 feet apart. Water moderately. Propagate from seed or cuttings or by layering. Creeping raspberry is hardy in Zones 7 to 9. Nepalese raspberry is hardy only to Zone 9.

GLOSSARY

APHID: A tiny, pear-shaped insect that sucks sap; typically pale green, gray, or yellowish-pink, and found in great numbers at tender growing points; secretes a sticky ant-attracting fluid called honeydew.

AQUATIC PLANT: A plant that grows in or on water.

BACILLUS THURINGIENSIS (BT): A bacteria used as a biological insecticide; kills caterpillars.

BENEFICIAL INSECT: An insect that aids gardening efforts by pollinating flowers, eating or parasitizing harmful insects, or breaking down organic material in the soil. Some insects are both harmful and beneficial, such as butterflies that pollinate plants as adults but can be destructive in their larval form.

BRACT: A leaf that looks like a flower. Many plants, such as bougainvillea, have colorful bracts and inconspicuous real flowers.

BROADCASTING: Sowing seed or applying fertilizer by scattering it across an area.

BUD: A dormant, embryonic shoot from which leaves or flowers grow.

CLIMBER: A plant with tendrils, or twining stems, aerial roots, or other physical method of attaching itself to structures or other plants.

COMPLETE FERTILIZER: A plant food that contains nitrogen, phosphorus, and potassium.

COMPOST: Decomposed organic matter used to improve both the texture and fertility of garden soil.

CONIFER: A cone-bearing tree with needle-like leaves.

CULTIVAR: A variety raised strictly through horticultural processes rather than occurring naturally; typically propagated from cuttings.

CULTIVATE: The process of breaking up the soil surface, removing weeds, and preparing the ground for planting.

DEADHEADING: The removal of spent flowers from a plant to prolong bloom. For effective results, the ovary behind the flower must be removed as well.

DECIDUOUS: Plants that lose all their leaves for part of the year.

DORMANCY: An annual period in a plant's life when growth slows and the plant rests.

EVERGREEN: A plant that remains green year-round because never loses all of its leaves.

FLAT: A shallow box or tray used by the greenhouse industry to hold cuttings or seedlings.

FOLIAR FEEDING: Applying a fine mist containing diluted soluble fertilizer directly to a plant's leaves.

FROND: Leafy stems of a fern.

FUNGICIDE: A material that kills fungi.

GERMINATION: The process of a seed sprouting.

GROWING SEASON: The number of days between the average dates of the last killing frost in spring and the first killing frost in fall.

HARDENING OFF: Exposing seedlings to outdoor conditions before transplanting.

HERBACEOUS: Plants that die back to the ground in winter.

INSECTICIDAL SOAP: A specially formulated mild soap that kills insects primarily by causing their outer shell to crack.

INSECTICIDE: A material that kills insects.

INVASIVE PLANTS: A plant that grows aggressively and spreads beyond its original site.

NATURALIZED: A landscape designed to resemble a natural setting.

NUTRIENT: Any substance essential for plant growth.

ORGANIC MATTER: Any material that originated as a living organism, such as peat moss, compost, and manure.

PEAT MOSS: Partially decomposed remains of bog mosses, which improves water-holding capacity of soil and may increase acidity.

PERENNIAL: A plant that lives more than three years.

PINCHING: The removal of a growing tip from a stem, thus causing axillary shoots or buds of the stem to develop.

RHIZOME: A thick, horizontal, underground stem from which buds and roots develop.

ROOT-BOUND: When plant roots have overfilled the pot in which they grow so that further growth is prevented or stunted.

ROOTING HORMONE: A powdered or liquid plant growth hormone that promotes the development of roots on a cutting.

SCARIFICATION: Breaking a hard, outer seed coat to promote germination.

SHEARING: Pruning wholesale, rather than individual stems; giving the plant a uniform outline.

SIDEDRESSING: Applying fertilizer to the soil surface around a plant.

SPECIES: The basic unit of plant classification. Plants in a species share characteristics and usually can cross with one another but rarely with plants of other species.

SPORE: The reproductive cell of ferns, fungi, and mosses. (These plants do not have seeds.)

STOLON: A horizontal stem that runs along the surface of the soil, rooting where its tip contacts the soil. A runner.

SUCCULENT: A plant with thick, fleshy, water-retaining leaves or stems.

THINNING: Removing excess seedlings from a bed or an area to make room for remaining plants. Thinning also refers to removing branches from a tree or shrub to open it up.

TUBER: An underground storage organ that is part of a plant's stem or root system.

VARIEGATED: Leaves marked with stripes, splotches, or dots of colors other than green.

VARIETY: A plant with distinct features that carry through successive generations in the absence of human intervention. Generally, variety applies to naturally occurring populations in specific geographic regions. Seeds breed true.

VEGETATIVE PROPAGATION: Increasing plant stock from vegetative parts of the plant, which normally results in a identical individuals. It may occur naturally through or be accomplished horticulturally from cuttings, division, budding, grafting, or layering.

XERISCAPE: A landscape that conserves water and protects the environment. Most xerophytic—drought-tolerant—plants need only minimal supplemental water after they are established, except during extreme drought.

THE USDA PLANT HARDINESS ZONE MAP OF NORTH AMERICA

Plants are classified according to the amount of cold weather they can handle. For example, a plant listed as hardy to zone 6 will survive a winter in which the temperature drops to minus 10° F.

Warm weather also influences whether a plant will survive in your region. Although this map does not address heat hardiness, in general, if a range of hardiness zones is listed for a plant, the plant will survive winter in the coldest zone as well as tolerate the heat of the warmest zone.

To use this map, find the location of your community, then match the color band marking that area to the zone key at left.

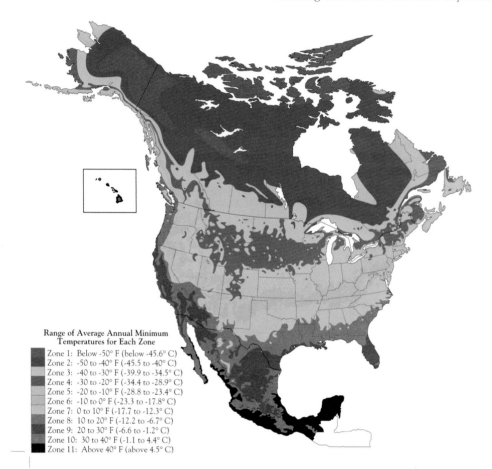

Range of Average Annual Minimum Temperatures for Each Zone

Zone 1: Below -50° F (below -45.6° C)
Zone 2: -50 to -40° F (-45.5 to -40° C)
Zone 3: -40 to -30° F (-39.9 to -34.5° C)
Zone 4: -30 to -20° F (-34.4 to -28.9° C)
Zone 5: -20 to -10° F (-28.8 to -23.4° C)
Zone 6: -10 to 0° F (-23.3 to -17.8° C)
Zone 7: 0 to 10° F (-17.7 to -12.3° C)
Zone 8: 10 to 20° F (-12.2 to -6.7° C)
Zone 9: 20 to 30° F (-6.6 to -1.2° C)
Zone 10: 30 to 40° F (-1.1 to 4.4° C)
Zone 11: Above 40° F (above 4.5° C)

METRIC CONVERSIONS

U.S. Units to Metric Equivalents			Metric Units to U.S. Equivalents		
To Convert From	Multiply By	To Get	To Convert From	Multiply By	To Get
Inches	25.4	Millimeters	Millimeters	0.0394	Inches
Inches	2.54	Centimeters	Centimeters	0.3937	Inches
Feet	30.48	Centimeters	Centimeters	0.0328	Feet
Feet	0.3048	Meters	Meters	3.2808	Feet
Yards	0.9144	Meters	Meters	1.0936	Yards

To convert from degrees Fahrenheit (F) to degrees Celsius (C), first subtract 32, then multiply by ⁵⁄₉.

To convert from degrees Celsius to degrees Fahrenheit, multiply by ⁹⁄₅, then add 32.